Date Due

"There never have been people who know but do not act. Those who are supposed to know but do not act simply do not yet know. . . . How can knowledge and action be separated?"

As a classic formulation of Neo-Confucian ethics, Wang Yang-ming's doctrine of the unity of knowledge and action dominated Chinese philosophy during the Ming dynasty and has fascinated scholars since. This essay aims at a plausible explication of Wang's doctrine in light of present inquiry concerning the relation between moral thought and action. It offers a critical sketch of fundamental elements in the transformation of learning into practice, including the creative and reflective aspects of moral agency and commitment, and it reformulates the doctrine in a contemporary idiom, using the insights of modern ethical theorists to show more clearly both the philosophical and the practical import of the doctrine.

Grasping the significance of Wang's doctrine, however, is also to understand properly its vision of an ideal harmony between man and nature. This vision at the heart of Wang's psychology is approached by means of a hypothesis concerning the language of Confucian vision. The hypothesis is applied to Wang's own remarks on the nature of *tao* and *jen*, and through this analysis an evaluation of Wang's contribution to moral psychology emerges. Here the notion of *reasonableness* is seen as central to Wang's endeavor and to Confucian ethics in general.

A. S. Cua is professor of philosophy at the Catholic University of America.

*The Unity
of Knowledge
and Action*

The Unity of Knowledge and Action

A STUDY IN WANG YANG-MING'S MORAL PSYCHOLOGY

A. S. Cua

THE UNIVERSITY PRESS OF HAWAII • *Honolulu*

MANUFACTURED IN THE UNITED STATES OF AMERICA

Library of Congress Cataloging in Publication Data

Cua, A. S. (Antonio S.), 1932–
The unity of knowledge and action.

Bibliography: p.
Includes index.
1. Wang, Yang-ming, 1472–1529—Ethics.
2. Ethics—History—16th century. I. Title.
B5234.W367C8   170'.92'4   81-23060
ISBN 0-8248-0786-3   AACR2

To my wife
Shoke-Hwee Khaw,
whose life exemplifies
chih-hsing ho-i

Contents

Analytical Table of Contents

Preface

This inquiry deals with Wang Yang-ming's doctrine of the unity of knowledge and action as a case study in the problem of moral commitment and achievement. My principal aim is to offer a critical sketch of some fundamental elements in Wang's moral psychology. After a preliminary examination of Wang's own elucidation of the general nature of his doctrine (Chapter 1), I turn to the volitional and intellectual aspects (Chapter 2) and in particular to the role of moral reflection in the actualization of the Confucian vision within the natural world (Chapter 3). The pedagogical aspect of Wang's doctrine is also considered (Chapter 4). In the concluding sections, I attempt to formulate a hypothesis concerning the language of Confucian vision as a way of approaching the question of evaluation. I suggest that the Confucian vision, to be properly evaluated, involves a recognition of the notion of reasonableness or the various qualities deemed necessary to our ascription of reasonableness to persons—a notion which I see as an inherent feature in the Confucian language of vision. It is hoped that this discussion of reasonableness will pave the way to a final assessment of Confucian ethics in general.

An earlier version of Chapter 1 was presented as a lecture at the College of Plattsburgh, State University of New York, on May 1, 1980, and at the meetings of the International Society for Chinese Philosophy at the College of Charleston,

Charleston, South Carolina, on June 11, 1980. In pursuing this project I have received valuable advice and encouragement from Professors Wing-tsit Chan, Chung-ying Cheng, Paul Weiss, and Eliot Deutsch. Dean Jude P. Dougherty, School of Philosophy, the Catholic University of America, has been supportive in providing for secretarial and graduate assistance. Mrs. Bonnie Kennedy and Paul Yamada have been most helpful in preparing this work for publication. To my daughter Athene I am deeply grateful for her care and concern while the writing was in progress. I am also grateful to Don Yoder for rendering invaluable suggestions in the final revision of the manuscript; and to Columbia University Press for permission to reprint excerpts from Wing-tsit Chan's translation of Wang Yang-ming, *Instructions for Practical Living and Other Neo-Confucian Writings*, published in 1963.

Introduction

The problem of justification of moral beliefs and actions has occupied a central place in contemporary moral philosophy. Until recent years, the inquiry has proceeded largely along epistemological routes. It was commonly assumed that so long as there exist rationally acceptable criteria for assessing claims to moral knowledge, moral actions are subject to the same criteria. Apart from the disputed status of claims to moral knowledge, the plausibility of the assumption depends on an adequate account of the nature of action and agency. In the first place, assessment of an action as good or bad, right or wrong, depends on one's conception of the action in question and, more generally, on an adequate characterization of human action. As Austin points out, "It is proper to consider first what is meant by, and what not, and what is included under, and what not, the expression 'doing an action' or 'doing something.' "[1] A careful analysis of the concept of action may bring to light a complex machinery involving intelligence, appreciation of the situation, planning, decision, execution, and so forth.[2] Each of these aspects of action may be singled out for attention and appraisal. Our appraisal of action may thus differ from case to case. Even if there are rationally acceptable criteria for moral judgment, these criteria depend on selective attention to the aspects of actions. In the second place, if we view an action as a reflection of an agent's moral character, it is essential that we understand first such notions as intention, motive, and perhaps will, as well as the general nature and role of moral knowledge or commitment in the exercise of moral agency.[3] Attention to this basic concern in philosophical psychology—in the broad sense as inclusive of philosophy of mind and the theory of action—has been a prominent feature in certain recent works in moral philosophy.[4]

In the interest of exploring the relation between moral philosophy and philosophical psychology, or more concisely moral psychology,[5] Wang Yang-ming's doctrine of the unity of moral knowledge and action *(chih-hsing ho-i)* offers excellent materials for a case study.[6] In the *Instructions*[7] his varying remarks elucidating the doctrine display a clear concern with mental states (such as desires and thoughts) and mental acts (such as will, thinking, and discrimination). Wang's notions are not always free from ambiguity, and the problem of explicating his key notions appears to be more than just a problem of interpretative translation. Disambiguation through reliance on the relevant portions of Wang's works is also required, as well as attention to the difficulties that are inherent in any attempt at a systematic formulation of a moral psychology.

This study is an inquiry into the possibility of a coherent and plausible, though admittedly partial, reconstruction of Wang's moral psychology. Such a task inevitably involves an abstraction of an aspect of Wang's philosophy for independent examination and, more particularly, a dissociation from Wang's comprehensive philosophy of mind *(hsin)* and his more or less distinctive conception of innate knowledge of the good *(liang-chih)*.[8] In so doing, I have taken Carsun Chang's statement seriously that Wang's doctrine of the unity of moral knowledge and action "does not necessarily have anything to do with monism (e.g., Wang's metaphysics of mind). It has a value in its own right, and a thinker who opposes the doctrine of monism may still subscribe to it."[9]

There is a dual advantage in this approach. On the one hand, we leave open the question of the connection between this doctrine and other aspects of Wang's philosophy, thus maintaining a neutral attitude vis-à-vis the status of this doctrine within his total philosophy.[10] More important, Wang's insights and difficulties regarding the nature of moral knowledge and action can be exhibited and reconsidered as a step toward an assessment of the doctrine's contribution to moral psychology. The present study can only be viewed as preliminary to these larger questions. It must be noted, however, that the bracketing of other aspects of Wang's philosophy is not an absolute one, for in the course of my explication I make use of certain remarks that pertain to these other aspects. But on the whole, I have been concerned with minimal interpretation, relatively independent of metaphysical issues.

1 The Problem and General Statement

1.1   Before proceeding to Wang's general statement on the unity
of moral knowledge and action, let me attend to what is plausibly *the* underlying question and offer some observations on
the status of the doctrine. The question of the relation between moral knowledge and action may be viewed as a
special aspect of the more general question concerning the
relation between practical knowledge and action; and this
question depends on a distinction between practical and intellectual or theoretical knowledge. One of the peculiar features of practical knowledge lies in its *claim* or influence on
action. The claim at issue, unlike the truth-claims implicit in
the notion of theoretical knowledge, expresses essentially a
demand on action. Practical knowledge, of course, has a cognitive content, and this content can be formulated in terms of
a set of statements amenable to theoretical treatment. But
much of our practical knowledge is knowledge-how which,
for the most part, is inchoate, and thus an agent may have it
without being able to articulate his knowledge in a coherent
way—say, in terms of a set of rules of skill. In the sense of having a claim on action rather than content, practical knowledge requires elucidation. This problem of elucidation becomes clearer when it is seen as a question of understanding
the moving power or *actuating force* or *import* of practical
knowledge. And this question is quite distinct from the question of justification, which pertains to the cognitive content
rather than to the actuating force of practical knowledge.[1]

Moral knowledge, however we describe or justify its content, is a form of practical knowledge in the sense of possessing an actuating import. Nonetheless, the question of the relation between moral knowledge and action, when focused on its cognitive content, can be construed as a question of the content's relevance to practice—that is, a question of application. For a moral theorist, it is important to attend to the possible conditions of application; and, when the cognitive content is regarded as a body of rules or principles, the question then turns on the application of these rules to particular situations. In one sense, this question is an engineering question, concerned, as it were, with devising appropriate techniques of applying rules. It can be observed that when the question is one of application, a preference for the cognitive content is already presupposed. And when the relation of moral knowledge to action is construed in this way, the task, though pragmatic in intent, can easily be pursued as an intellectual enterprise. When this happens, instead of engaging in actual practice, one can remain on the intellectual plane. The danger here is simply that of converting practical to intellectual knowledge.

1.2   I suggest that the question underlying Wang's doctrine of the unity of moral knowledge and action pertains essentially to understanding the actuating import rather than the cognitive content of moral knowledge. But the question of understanding here, though distinct from the question of justification, is hardly intelligible apart from the content. Moreover, there may be an interaction between the actuating force and the content of moral knowledge that has interesting ramifications for our understanding of the nature of moral agency.

At this juncture, one can quite properly ask for a criterion for distinguishing the content of moral knowledge from that of other forms of practical knowledge. If Wang were confronted with this query, one assumes that he, as a Confucian, would appeal to the standard Confucian *aretaic notions* or various notions of virtues.[2] The distinctive content of moral knowledge would then consist of the requirements expressed in such notions as filiality *(hsiao)*, ritual propriety *(li)*, righteousness *(i)*, and humanity *(jen)*. More generally, the distinction between moral and nonmoral knowledge lies in the basic contrast between a concern for one's own and other persons' virtuous character and an exclusive concern for personal gain or self-interest.[3] In Wang, this contrast often appears in the form of a disjunction between moral knowledge and private desires *(szu yü)*.

Paying heed to the cognitive content, we can now view the actuating force of moral knowledge more perspicuously as a question which has to do with the actuating force of Confucian aretaic notions. Since the Confucian agent, for the most part, learns the use of these notions from parents, teachers, and others, his moral knowledge is largely derived from the cultural tradition. The question can thus also appear as one concerning the actuating force of moral learning. The question is especially a *live* and difficult one for a moral teacher such as Wang. Apart from the difficulty of inculcating a critical attitude toward existing conventions governing conduct and training the pupils in compliance with moral requirements, there is more crucially the problem of getting the pupils to *see* the actuating force of these requirements.[4] The task here is both pedagogical and moral. As a moral agent, the teacher is precluded from an appeal to physical coercion or rhetorical tricks, for these are means of deception incompatible with being sincere. They also amount to self-deception. Thus the *Great Learning (Ta-hsüeh)* points out that "making the will sincere" is allowing no self-deception.[5] The problem of moral teaching is, in this sense, also a problem of moral agency. Evidently, it is a source of persistent concern because of the recurrent experience of moral failure in both teaching and the exercise of moral agency.

1.3   If the preceding discussion of the question underlying Wang's
       doctrine of the unity of moral knowledge and action is
       deemed plausible, then the doctrine cannot be regarded as an
       attempt at a straightforward exposition of the cognitive con-
       tent of moral knowledge in relation to action. Wang is ob-
       viously quite aware that one can be said to know that such-
       and-such an action ought to be done, and yet that person can
       fail to do so. As we shall see shortly, these reasons for failure,
       according to Wang, are private or selfish desires. Nor can the
       doctrine be viewed as a doctrine in normative ethics, for
       Wang does not show much concern with providing specific
       norms or criteria as guides to both moral deliberation and the
       appraisal of actual conduct. In light of his conception of *tao*,
       it may be said to be an adumbration of a moral ideal.[6] But
       such an ideal is more a *theme*, a perspective for orientation
       toward the changing scenes of human life, than a norm for
       assessing policies of action.[7] It is perhaps best to take up this
       topic after an examination of Wang's arguments and exam-
       ples in the course of elucidating his doctrine of the unity of
       moral knowledge and action [2.13–2.14]. In what follows,
       with this exposition of the underlying question as back-
       ground, I center my attention on his relevant conversations
       with *Hsü Ai* (sec. 5 of *Instructions*) and will consider a series
       of apparently compendious but incisive remarks as a step to-
       ward a coherent and plausible explication of the doctrine.

1.4   As a point of departure, let me make explicit an assumption
       regarding the key terms and their alleged relations. I shall
       construe *chih* as moral knowledge (henceforth, knowledge) in
       the sense already explained [1.3]—that is, as practical knowl-
       edge with a content that has an actuating import. I leave
       open the question of whether the aretaic notions can be re-
       stated in terms of moral principles or whether they are
       merely guidelines open to different interpretations in different
       circumstances. The notion of *hsing* I simply render as moral

action, a deed or an actual moral performance. There is, of course, a certain ambiguity in Wang's uses of *chih* and *hsing*, but for my purpose the ambiguity constitutes a problem for coherent explication rather than a basis of criticism.

The doctrine of the unity *(ho-i)* of knowledge and action is a conception of the relation between two notions which, in abstraction from this relation, would refer to two different things or "states of affairs" *(wu)*. Apart from Wang, one can, by attending to the cognitive content alone, view that relation as a relation between two independent things. So construed, the relation between the two items would be an external one. But since Wang's doctrine is obviously directed against this view, what he has in mind is some sort of *internal* relation; the doctrine is then more plausibly concerned with the actuating import of the cognitive content of moral knowledge in actual performance. We may say that the relation between knowledge and action is an *internal* and not an external relation; the problem of explication lies in plausibly articulating this internal relation. The relation, however, is not a logically necessary one. On the face of it, it is more like a kinship relation between persons. At any rate, a unitary relation between knowledge and action suggests clearly that both are distinct but intimately connected. As I shall later elaborate, for pedagogical purposes legitimate abstraction is allowed in certain circumstances [4.1]. What the doctrine denies is the dichotomy or exclusive disjunction between knowledge and action. That Wang explicitly recognizes this distinction is evident in a letter to a friend: "Knowledge and action are really two words describing the same effort. This one effort requires these two words in order to be explained completely."[8] Another remark of Wang further suggests a rather interesting attitude toward distinctions in general— that is, the attitude that a conceptual distinction is often intelligible because of the connection between the items at issue. In commenting on the passage (in the *Great Learning*) that "things have their roots and their branches," Wang states that "the main thing is that root and branches should not be distinguished as two different (and independent) things. The trunk of the tree is called the root, and the twigs are called the branches. It is precisely because the tree is one that its parts can be called root and branches."[9]

1.5   Consider now Wang's general statement (*Instructions*, sec. 5). In response to the observation that "there are people who know that parents should be served with filial piety and elder brothers with respect but cannot put these things into practice," Wang states that "the knowledge and action you refer to are already separated by selfish desires and are no longer knowledge and action in their original substance *(pen-ti)*. There have never been people who know but do not act. Those who are supposed to know but do not act simply do not yet know." What I call Wang's general statement is the view that the *pen-ti* ("original substance") of knowledge and action is a unity. Postponing for a moment his view of selfish desires, let us proceed directly to Wang's elucidation. For convenience, I shall label the two components "aesthetic analogy" and "psychological analogy."

1.6   The *aesthetic analogy* occurs in the following:

Passage A:
The *Great Learning* points to true knowledge and action for people to see, saying, they are "like loving beautiful colors and hating bad odors." *Seeing* beautiful colors appertains to knowledge, while *loving* beautiful colors appertains to action. However, as soon as one sees that beautiful color, he has already loved it.

Passage B:
Suppose we say that so-and-so *knows* filial piety and so-and-so knows brotherly respect. They must have actually practiced filial piety and brotherly respect before they can be said to know them.

It will not do to *say* that they know filial piety and brotherly respect simply because they show them in words.[10]

Instead of ascribing to Wang a doctrine of sense perception,[11] let us confine our attention to his example of what might be called aesthetic perception. Seeing beautiful colors or objects in general may be said to involve a *conative* attitude. As a way of making explicit the attitude, we may replace "seeing beautiful colors" by "seeing colors *as* beautiful." If we attribute a capacity of discrimination to the person, we may say that this discrimination is tied to his disposition to love an object of similar description. There is no need to attribute to him a conscious decision to see the object in this way. As soon as one sees an object as beautiful, one has already loved it in the sense that one has spontaneously responded to the object as a beautiful object. The object of our aesthetic perception is a "proper" object in that we do not have to reflect on its nature prior to the response. Our response may appear deliberate without our having gone through a process of deliberation.[12] For our purpose, we need not inquire into the question of whether all cases of aesthetic perception can be treated in this way. But what we need to understand in the example is some notion of "seeing as" or "aspect-seeing." Wittgenstein reminds us that " 'seeing as . . .' is not part of perception. And for that reason it is like seeing and again not like." Sometimes we can look at something without seeing it in the aspectual sense. And when we see an object as an object of a certain description, it simply *dawns* on us.[13] In the aesthetic case, the conative attitude or disposition may well be a by-product of our aesthetic education. And in a situation where a normally beautiful object is present without our noticing it as such, we may be said to be aesthetically blind—that is, experiencing a failure in aesthetic perception.[14]

If this interpretation of Wang's example is acceptable, there is still a problem of understanding Wang's claim that seeing beautiful colors belongs to knowledge *(chih)* and loving beautiful colors belongs to action *(hsing)*. Wang's notion of action here refers to *reflexive response* rather than action proper, which refers to deed or actual performance [1.4] and is clearly the notion appealed to in passage B. As to the notion of knowledge, it is in some way related to the notion of "seeing as." Here knowledge would be a state of recognition—that is, direct awareness of an object as having a certain quality. Thus if I am directly aware of, or recognize, an object *X* as beautiful, I may be properly said to know *X* in Russell's sense of *knowledge by acquaintance* as distinct from knowledge by description.[15] But whether moral knowledge is akin to knowledge by acquaintance turns on the plausibility of the analogy alleged in passage B.

1.7   The intended analogy in passage B seems to be this: Just as seeing an object *X* as beautiful is already to have a loving response to *X*, knowing filial piety or brotherly respect is already to have practiced filial piety and brotherly respect. If we confine our attention to the knowing aspect, in both cases some knowledge by acquaintance seems involved. As in the aesthetic case, when I am directly aware of, or recognize, a person *A* as my father or my brother, I may be said to have already "responded" to *A* in the way characteristic of a filial son or respectful brother; that is, I have already *acted* toward *A* in a filial or fraternal way. But the notion of response here is an action, as we noted above, and is distinct from a mere reflexive response. Thus we have but a partial analogy. We have a full analogy only when we grant Wang's equivocation on the notion of *hsing*—that is, as mere reflexive response and as human action. Also, in the moral case mere knowledge by acquaintance is not enough. The sense of recognition involved is more a sense of *acknowledgment*.[16] The analogy is illuminating only in showing that there is no gap, properly speaking, between acknowledging *A*, in the normative sense, as my father and acting toward *A* in the filial way.[17]

If we set aside the difficulty with Wang's notion of action, passage B suggests quite clearly the notion of moral knowledge as a species of practical knowledge [1.1]. One can, of course, attend exclusively to the cognitive content of moral knowledge apart from its actuating import. But in doing so one is merely manifesting an intellectual curiosity. Even if a person can ably engage in discourse about morality, thereby exemplifying his verbal knowledge of the uses of moral notions, this does not show that he is in possession of moral knowledge in the sense of *understanding* or appreciating its actuating import. Intellectual knowledge of morality does not amount to moral knowledge. Having moral knowledge in the required sense involves not merely a recognition that such-and-such is a duty but also an *acknowledgment* or acceptance of the duty as a guide to actual conduct—that is, as having an actuating import in one's life. This acknowledgment also involves, as in the aesthetic case, a conative attitude or endeavor to perform the dutiful act, though unlike the aesthetic case, the endeavor is conscious and active. If I acknowledge, for example, filial piety as my duty, this involves not merely a recognition of what constitutes acts of filial piety but also an endeavor to perform these acts. Unlike the aesthetic case, however, the absence of the gap is the result of my successful moral endeavor—that is, in the actual practice of deeds of filial piety. In a sense moral failure is like aesthetic blindness. The obstruction of selfish desires can result in moral failure just as in the case of aesthetic failure or "aspect blindness." Thus I may fail to see a current object as beautiful because of my nonaesthetic interests (economic, prudential, even moral). The point is not that we do not see the object in the visual sense but that we do not see it *as* possessing certain aesthetic qualities. In the moral case, we can also speak of moral blindness in the metaphorical sense, and in this sense selfish desires can have a blinding effect upon our understanding of the actuating import of moral knowledge.

In focusing on selfish desires as a sole explanation of moral failure, Wang has neglected other factors. Clearly one may also fail because of the lack of opportunity or means for carrying out the duty of filial piety or because of conflict of duties or circumstances beyond our control. But in the case of moral achievement, Wang is incisive in reminding us that moral knowledge cannot be properly *ascribed* to a person unless there is evidence of moral action. The proper uses of aretaic notions for ascribing moral qualities to persons depend for their appeal on virtuous performance [1.2]. A man cannot be properly called a "filial son" unless he has performed filial acts. When we construe moral qualities in dispositional terms, these qualities can be ascribed only on the basis of practice, for what counts as a moral disposition depends on the actual manifestation of the disposition in conduct. More particularly, in one's own case, the ability to use aretaic notions has no necessary connection with one's entitlement to the possession of moral qualities. Moral knowledge as related to achievement is, in Ryle's terms, *operative* rather than *academic* knowledge—a notion, I believe, that can be rendered intelligible when we turn to what I call the psychological analogy.[18]

1.8   The *psychological analogy* occurs in the following passage:

> *Passage C:*
> Or take one's knowledge of pain. Only after one has experienced pain can one know pain. The same is true of cold and hunger. How can knowledge *(chih)* and action *(hsing)* be separated?

I take this remark, which immediately follows passage B, as an attempt to elucidate moral knowledge as a form of achievement. That moral knowledge, in terms of its actuating import, is wedded to actual moral practice is a thesis that is intelligible and plausible. This we have considered relative to passage B. The intended analogy here, on the other hand, appears to be a decisive move to elucidate the unity of knowledge and action. Initially, this move is rather puzzling, for the analogy with one's knowledge of mental states such as feelings of pain, hunger, or cold at most points to the role of personal experience in moral knowledge—a recurrent theme in Wang's philosophy. How this is possible is far from clear. If we make use of our earlier discussion of aesthetic perception, it is unproblematic to regard the knowledge at issue as a form of knowledge by acquaintance or recognition [1.6]. But we have also noted that moral knowledge is more a form of acknowledgment with regard to understanding the import of its cognitive content in actual practice. If passage C is to throw more light on this form of acknowledgment, then it must be construed as emphasizing personal experience as a source of moral knowledge. In other words, I am now able to recognize the actuating import of moral knowledge because I have in fact personally experienced it in action. But obviously one can also understand the actuating import of moral knowledge, *prior* to actual practice, from sources other than personal experience—for example, from teachers, elders, or fellow agents [1.2]. An appreciation of the actuating import does not entail that the import is actually experienced, though such an experience does sometimes affect our appreciation. It is this function of experience, aiding our appreciation of the actuating import of moral knowledge, that lies at the heart of passage C.

1.9   In order to capture Wang's insight, let us consider two senses of moral knowledge in respect of its actuating import. Prior to actual performance, I may have an understanding of the actuating import of such virtues as filial piety and humility. Such an understanding consists simply in an acknowledgment of the actuating import of these moral requirements. Though this acknowledgment is not a verbal matter, it signifies an acceptance of moral knowledge as a guide to *my* life. Moral knowledge, in other words, has significance for me because I accept its content as a guide to my actual conduct. If I do not pay heed to its requirements, barring insincerity, I have failed to appreciate what it is to be a virtuous agent. But in a certain sense I do not *truly* understand the actuating import until I have acted in accordance with the requirements. Just as I cannot truly understand that another person is in pain until I have actually experienced pain, I do not truly understand what it is to be a filial son until I have actually acted in the filial way—that is, performed deeds of filial piety. So there appears to be a distinction between two different sorts of understanding. In focusing on this distinction, we may thus distinguish moral knowledge that is *anterior to action* from moral knowledge that is *posterior to action*.[19] Since the former has a prospective and the latter a retrospective significance, we may call them "prospective" and "retrospective" moral knowledge, respectively.

Prospective moral knowledge, being anterior to action, is an acknowledgment of the *projective* significance of moral requirements as a guide to one's life. It anticipates the character of moral experience. Such an anticipation can be frustrated in the course of moral endeavor and, for Wang, by the constant insistence of self-interested concern or selfish desires [1.7]. Self-interest, aside from being a potential source of conflict with moral requirements, has a tendency to obscure *(pi)* our understanding of the actuating import of moral knowledge. When understanding is unobscured and followed by appropriate action, it will eventuate in retrospective moral knowledge. It is a personal moral experience, an experience derived from encounter and participation in human affairs. For the Confucian, this consists largely in the experience of human relationships *(lun)* in the varying circumstances of one's moral life. When such an experience occurs, it need not take a self-consciously reflective or intellectual form. As

Wang succinctly points out, "Knowledge acquired through personal realization is different from that acquired through listening to discussion."[20] There are times when the realization can occur without our awareness, but Wang adds that "if we don't know this we will be lost."[21]

This experience or personal realization of prospective moral knowledge may be said to be a demonstration of one's genuine understanding *(chen-chih)* as contrasted with the relatively shallow understanding in acknowledging the actuating import of moral requirements prior to action.[22] In conceptual terms we may construe Wang's focus on personal experience as an emphasis on understanding the import rather than the meaning of moral notions. The import of moral notions lies in the use of moral language as it has a transformative significance for the life of the speaker.[23] Of course, for Wang this sort of understanding is a culmination of "an experiential understanding of the teaching of [Confucian] sages"[24] and not an insight derived from conceptual investigation.

1.10   Equipped with this distinction between prospective and retrospective knowledge, let us turn to two famous compendious remarks on the unity of knowledge and action:

> *Passage D:*
> Knowledge is the direction of action and action the effort of knowledge.

> *Passage E:*
> Knowledge is the beginning of action and action the completion of knowledge.

Wang continues: "If this is understood, then when only knowledge is mentioned, action is included, and when only action is mentioned, knowledge is included."[25] Let us consider passages D and E, first separately and then together, and see whether or not we have a coherent and plausible doctrine.

The notion of knowledge in passage D is prospective rather than retrospective moral knowledge. As prospective knowledge, by virtue of its cognitive content [1.2], it provides a *direction* to actual conduct. Since Wang's use of *chu-yi* can also be rendered as "leading idea," the first half of passage D can thus be restated: "Prospective moral knowledge, by virtue of its cognitive content, is a leading idea of action." Since the use of *kung-fu*, apart from effort, can also be rendered as work or accomplishment, the second half of passage D can be restated as "action is the work or accomplishment of prospective knowledge," in the sense of successful effort devoted to carrying out moral requirements. Effort is involved in prospective moral knowledge, for this knowledge, as we have observed, is an acknowledgment of the actuating import of moral requirements [1.7]. The acknowledgment is an acceptance that also involves a conative attitude in the sense of an effort to carry out, say, one's duty in actual conduct. The point can alternatively be put in terms of the notion of commitment. We can say that if one is aware of one's moral commitment, and if this commitment is serious, then one must show the seriousness by expending actual effort. The hope is to be successful in the effort. And when one attains this achievement, one can also be said to have retrospective moral knowledge, which is a focus of passage E.

In passage E, both senses of moral knowledge appear to be involved. Prospective knowledge is the beginning of action, and action is the completion or achievement of this knowledge, but the knowledge is retrospective. Using the point in passage D, prospective knowledge is a task and retrospective knowledge is an accomplishment, or the experience of actual practice. If we regard the cognitive content of prospective knowledge as a by-product of learning, we may conceive of passages D and E together as putting forth a conception of moral learning. Moral learning, if it is deemed successful, is learning that has a transformative effect in the student's life.

The moral requirements—the cognitive content of moral knowledge—are a component of the moral life. When such learning has been fulfilled in the moral life, we have retrospective knowledge of the course of our moral experience. This is what it means to become a *moral agent*. Thus passages D and E together can be viewed as a plausible attempt at an elucidation of moral agency and, more particularly, as a doctrine concerning the proper ascription of the successful exercise of moral agency [1.7].

1.11   Passages D and E differ in emphasis, however, if we focus on mere effort rather than successful effort or retrospective moral knowledge. In this light, while passage D stresses the process, passage E stresses the moral achievement. The process for Wang is not a temporal process consisting of discrete stages ordered in terms of before and after but a *continuum* of prospective moral knowledge through successful efforts eventuating in retrospective moral knowledge.[26] This continuum of moral knowledge and action may also be more succinctly stated as the "original substance" *(pen-ti)* that expresses the *intrinsic nature* of both knowledge and action —or, if one prefers, the noncontingent connection between prospective and retrospective moral knowledge. It is a noncontingent connection in that both moral knowledge and action are mutually dependent notions.[27] Prospective moral knowledge involves the expense of actual effort. When the effort is successful, our action is in retrospect an accomplishment of what we set out to do in accord with prospective moral knowledge. When the effort fails—owing, for example, to the interference of selfish desires—our moral knowledge and action become separated. When this occurs, we may end up in two separate and independent pursuits.

For pedagogical purposes, particularly for the rectification of character defects, knowledge and action may be separately emphasized to restore their proper balance as twin aspects of the same moral process. But if one exclusively pursues the cognitive content regardless of its actuating import, one may, in Wang's words, be chasing after "shadows and echoes, as it were." Equally, if one focuses exclusively on actuating force without regarding the cognitive content, one is liable to become, according to Wang, "confused and act on impulse without any sense of deliberation or self-examination, and . . . thus also behave blindly and erroneously." The pursuit of moral knowledge, mindful of both cognitive content and its actuating import, is thus an intelligent and concerned, not an empty and irresponsible, occupation. Wang assures his pupils that his doctrine is not a product of baseless imagination but has the principal aim of being "a medicine for that disease" of separately pursuing moral knowledge and action [4.1–4.3].

1.12   This discussion of sec. 5 of *Instructions* offers, I hope, a plausible reconstruction of Wang's doctrine of the unity of moral knowledge and action. The reconstruction, however, sketches a larger terrain that requires a more detailed elaboration. If we attend primarily to retrospective knowledge or experience, questions quite naturally arise concerning the constitutive elements of such a moral achievement. In general, we may depict it as a culmination of a process of transition from prospective to retrospective knowledge and then inquire into the various elements involved in the successful exercise of moral agency. In the next chapter, I shall pursue this task by reflecting on Wang's further compendious remarks. In doing so, we may discover also the complexity and complications of Wang's moral psychology.

2 Further Complications: Volitional and Intellectual Acts

2.1   Prospective knowledge as acknowledgment is an expression of an *active* concern for the actuating import of moral requirements in particular circumstances. It is a regard for human affairs. If one were an official of a district, knowing would involve an active caring for all the affairs of the district as one's own affairs.[1] If it is to be free from blind and impulsive action, the effort must be informed and intelligent [1.11]. This means that one must *learn* to do such things as study, think, inquire, and sift. As Wang points out:

> No one really learns anything without carrying it into action. . . . And thus, in seeking to dispel doubts, we call it inquiry. In seeking to understand an idea of a doctrine [or moral requirements], we call it thinking. In seeking to examine the idea carefully, we call it sifting [or discrimination]. And in seeking to carry the idea out in actual practice, we call it doing. Speaking from the point of view of a combined affair [i.e., in light of the active concern], they are one.[2]

The transition from prospective to retrospective knowledge thus involves such mental acts as thinking, inquiry, and discrimination. Such activities, though inspired by moral concern, do not properly amount to moral action, for they can be done solely *in foro interno*.[3] Nevertheless, Wang's remark does point to an *intellectual* component in the progress toward retrospective knowledge or moral achievement. The emphasis on the unity of learning and doing *(hsüeh-hsing ho-i)* can thus be said to be an emphasis on the intellectual aspect of the unity of knowledge and action. This is as it should be, since the cognitive content of moral knowledge still has to be attended to with clarity. Deliberating on what one ought to do in a particular situation thus includes a component of intellectual reflection. At issue is not merely the relevance of intellectual knowledge to moral practice, but "the pondering or manipulation according to one's personal wishes" without any moral concern.[4] For other components, let us turn to Wang for guidance.

2.2   First let us attend to the following:

> *Passage F:*
> The master of the body is the mind. What emanates from the mind is *yi*. The original substance *(pen-ti)* of *yi* is knowledge, and wherever the *yi* is directed is a "thing" *(wu)*.[5]

The notion of *wu*, referring to "things," includes events, states of affairs, or more generally in light of Wang's moral interest, human affairs *(shih)*.[6] Wang continues:

> For example, when *yi* is directed toward serving one's parents, then serving one's parents is a "thing." . . . When *yi* is directed toward being humane *(jen)* to all people and feeling love toward things, then being humane to all people and feeling love toward things are "things," and when *yi* is directed toward seeing, hearing, speaking, and moving *(tung)*, then each of these is a "thing."[7]

Since action is an event, it also is a "thing." The difficulty, apart from Wang's notion of mind, which we shall discuss later [2.9], pertains to the notion of *yi*. In the present passage, we can follow Professor Chan by rendering it as will or volition. But other renderings have also been proposed, and some of these are supported by the text—for example, intention,[8] pure motive,[9] and desire.[10] The variety of possible renderings is a challenge for a coherent reconstruction, for all these renderings pertain to the complexity of the transition from prospective to retrospective knowledge. Before we take up this task, it must be observed that the expression "the original substance *(pen-ti)* of *yi* is knowledge" is sometimes rephrased by Wang as "the *yi* is knowledge in operation."[11] This knowledge is thus prospective in character, and it may simply be called operative knowledge [1.7].

2.3   When we regard *yi* as related to *chih**, as in the expression *yi-chih**, it can be rendered as will or volition. In a letter to his disciples, Wang stresses the importance of establishing one's will *(li-chih*)* or firm determination: "If the will is not [firmly] established, nothing in the world can be accomplished. Though there may be hundreds of professions, there is not a single one that does not depend on such a determination."[12] The function of the will *(chih*)* is brought out in the following: "When a good thought arises, recognize it and develop it fully. When an evil thought arises, recognize it and stop it. It is the will *(chih*)* that recognizes the thought and develops or stops it."[13] To borrow Reid's term, the will or volition is an *active power*—that is, the act of determining or "the determination of the mind to do or not to do something which we conceive to be within our power"—and, typically, "when we will to do a thing immediately, the volition is accompanied with an effort to execute that which we willed."[14] When the will is informed by the cognitive content of moral knowledge, it may thus be regarded as knowledge in operation. In effect, the will is a mediation between prospective knowledge and action or retrospective knowledge.

2.4   I do not mean to ascribe a special doctrine of volition to Wang's notion of *yi*, for all that is required is some notion of willing or resolution to carry out the moral requirements embedded in prospective knowledge. This mental act, as we have observed, does not constitute action in the proper sense [1.7].[15] Such a resolution can be seen as a resolve to form an intention appropriate to acting in accord with moral requirements. *Yi* can thus also be rendered as "intention." I cannot claim to know the actuating import of filiality unless I form an intention to act filially in a current situation. In other words, an acknowledgment of filiality is a commitment, which is a product of the will, to form appropriate intentions whenever filiality is deemed relevant to a situation. In intending to perform an action, I must be supposed to have some idea of what I am doing, though this need not be "so full-blooded as a plan proper."[16] Confronted with thoughts *(nein)*, as a concerned agent I pursue the good ones rather than the bad ones in accordance with appropriate moral requirements [2.3]. If I then succeed in carrying out my current intention, I have, in effect, transformed my prospective knowledge into retrospective knowledge. Again, *yi* can be regarded as a mediation, though as an agent's intention it pertains to an occurrent situation. The intention at issue is also expressive of my active concern for morality [2.1].

2.5 Seen in light of retrospective knowledge or moral achievement, *yi* can be explained as an outcome of a peculiar *moral motive*—that is, a successful expression of one's moral will. It is the sincerity of the will *(ch'eng-yi)* in the *Great Learning* to which Wang pays special attention.[17] It is the pursuit of the good with single-mindedness, "allowing no double-mindedness regardless of longevity or brevity of life."[18] This notion has a striking affinity to Kierkegaard's conception of purity of heart or will. "In truth," says Kierkegaard, "to will one thing . . . can only mean to will the Good, because every other object is not a unity; and the will that only wills that object, therefore, must become double-minded. For as the coveted object is, so becomes the coveter."[19] Like Wang, Kierkegaard is distrustful of efforts expended in the search for success, fame, and profit, which are external rather than an integral part of the moral pursuit.[20] *Yi*, as a will devoted to the highest good, is an emanation from the mind, and this highest good *(chih-shan)* is the original substance *(pen-ti)* of the mind.[21]

2.6   The preceding discussion of *yi* as will, intention, and motive is complicated by one remark of Wang that explicitly equates *yi* with desire. In a letter to a friend, Wang states that

> a man must have the desire *(yü)* for food before he knows the food. This desire to eat is *yi*; it is already the beginning of action. Whether the taste of the food is good or bad cannot be known until the food enters the mouth. . . . A man must have the desire *(yü)* to travel before he knows the road. This desire to travel is *yi*; it is already the beginning of action.[22]

Without critical interpolation, this problematic passage can hardly be viewed as consistent with the other senses of *yi*. While the knowledge in question is retrospective, it is not open to doubt. *Yi* cannot be construed as ordinary desire unless we make a distinction between first-order and second-order desires—that is, ordinary desire such as the desires to eat or to travel and typically moral desires or the general desire to do good. Frankfurt explains the notion of second-order desire in this way: "Someone has a desire of the second order either when he wants simply to have a certain desire or when he wants a certain desire to be his will." In the latter situation, we have "second-order volitions" or "volitions of a second order."[23] The possession of second-order desires presupposes "the capacity for reflective self-evaluation."[24] The notion of second-order desire seems implicit in a passage in *Hsün Tzu:* "A single desire which one receives from nature *(t'ien)* is regulated and directed by the mind in many different ways, and it is certainly difficult to identify it in terms of its original appearance."[25] If *yi* is to be plausibly construed as desire that is elucidative of the connection of moral knowledge and action, it must thus be qualified as a second-order moral desire in contrast with selfish desires, which are also desires of the second order. Since we are not concerned with textual exegesis but with plausible explication, *yi* should be construed as a second-order moral desire to do good or to realize the highest good if Wang is to avoid inconsistency.

2.7   If the preceding discussion of the notion of *yi* is deemed acceptable, we may now attempt a partial but coherent reformulation of Wang's doctrine of the unity of moral knowledge and action. As prospective, moral knowledge is acknowledgment; it is an expression of an active moral concern. An ingredient in such an expression is *will* or volition in the sense of a firm determination to do what is in one's power in compliance with moral requirements. And if such a will is to be effective in action, the agent must form appropriate *intentions* whenever these requirements are adjudged to be relevant to particular situations. For fulfilling these intentions, intellectual activities such as inquiry, thinking, and deliberation may have to be carried out [2.1]. But these intentions are formed out of the will to do good, which involves a second-order moral *desire*. Such a desire—or, more generally, the purity of one's moral *motive* in retrospective moral achievement—can also be invoked to explain the successful course of moral endeavor. The complexity of the notion of *yi* may thus be captured in a summary statement concerning the structure of the successful exercise of moral agency. At the same time, the statement focuses on *yi* as a mediation between prospective and retrospective moral knowledge.

The present scenario cannot pretend to be complete or even creditable, however, unless some account is given of the nature of the agent's involvement in the world via the intellectual route of moral reflection. For what is depicted thus far is, in effect, a psychological drama of the interior life. Were moral life to be so confined, it would be deprived of a connection with the outer world of other persons, objects, and events. It must be admitted that Wang, for the most part, puts a premium on the inward aspect of the moral life.[26] His attention to the outward aspect appears to be evident in an attempt to restate his doctrine in terms of the notion of *li** in one of his famous compendious remarks.

2.8   It is instructive to approach Wang's conception of *li** by taking brief note of his saying that "knowledge in its genuine and earnest aspect is action, and action in its intelligent and discerning aspect is knowledge."[27] In terms of our distinction between prospective and retrospective knowledge [1.9], we can more perspicuously set forth Wang's view by saying that "prospective knowledge, if it is serious, must be accompanied by effort to realize its objective in action; and action, if it is not to be blind, must be intelligently discerned as an object of retrospective knowledge."[28] Quite naturally, this view gives rise to a question concerning the nature of intelligent discernment.

2.9   Wang could reply to the question by maintaining that "knowledge is the intelligence *(ling-ming)* of the mind."[29] Or more fully:

> *Passage G:*
> Knowledge is the intelligent locus *(ling-ch'u)* of *li**. In terms of its position as the master [of the body], it is called mind. In terms of its position as endowment, it is called our nature.[30]

This passage suggests that human beings can be conceived in different ways from different points of view. These points of view function like focal lenses for giving emphasis to different aspects of human beings in varying contexts of discourse.

There are times, however, when two or more points of view are simultaneously deployed for displaying the connection between the different aspects. Looking back, for example, at our discussion of *yi* in passage G, what is portrayed is the connection between mind, knowledge, *yi*, and things [2.2]. That Wang has a monistic metaphysics, and more particularly a metaphysics with a moral focus, has been widely noted by scholars and philosophers. If my observation regarding different and complementary points of view is correct, then Wang's doctrine of the unity of knowledge and action can be regarded as a proper basis for explicating his philosophy as a whole. For the time being, let me simply offer this possibility as a suggestion and concentrate on the immediate problem.[31]

In the reconstruction thus far, the thesis that "knowledge is the intelligence of the mind" can be regarded as an ellipsis to be expanded in the following way. Intelligence *(ling-ming)* here pertains to keen and clear "perception." Prospectively, it is clear discernment of the relevance of moral requirements to a situation at hand. This is a clarity of mind with respect to the actuating import of moral knowledge. It implies especially the discernment of good and evil thoughts [2.3]. When this discernment is effectively manifested in action via *yi* as will, we may be said to have operative knowledge [2.2]. To be plausible, knowledge as intelligence must be construed as a mental act. In this respect, it differs from retrospective knowledge in that the latter is a mental state of intelligent awareness. Alternatively, it is a consummation of the successful effort to actualize the prospective knowledge—a consummatory moral experience with a noetic quality. This state of awareness is something that is enjoyed by a successful moral agent. In this light, joy may be said to be characteristic of "the original substance *(pen-ti)* of the mind."[32] It is a state in which the moral agent's mind is at home with his present condition.[33]

When we turn to passage G, we face a double perplexity:

What is *li**? And in what sense is knowledge the intelligent locus *(ling-ch'u)* of *li**? With respect to the second question, Wang offers us relatively clear guidance. He says that "when the intelligent faculty or capacity *(ling-neng)* is not obstructed by selfish desires, but is developed and extended to the limit, it is then completely the original substance of the mind and can identify its character with that of Heaven and Earth."[34] In this sense, "mind is *li** *(hsin-chi-li*)*" expresses a vision of the harmony of man and all things [2.12].[35] For the present, let us observe that the intelligent capacity is a capacity to acquire knowledge of *li**. More clearly, perhaps, to have retrospective knowledge is to be aware of *li** as its proper object. In this clarity of mind, that is, knowledge as achievement, knowledge is the intelligent locus of *li**.[36] Note that *ling*, which is rendered as "intelligence," can also be properly translated as "spirit." This, of course, is a more metaphorical rendering, but it is suggestive of knowledge or clarity of mind, which is where the spirit of *li** dwells. Put more simply, knowledge is the indwelling spirit of *li**. Whether this interpretation can be fully intelligible depends on an adequate answer to the prior question concerning the notion of *li**.

2.10   Like the notion of *yi*, *li** presents an interesting challenge for plausible reconstruction. The challenge, however, is a most difficult one to meet with confidence, because this key term in Neo-Confucianism has a long history of evolution and a variety of recent interpretations that almost defy any sympathetic attempt at a coherent statement.[37] For almost a decade I have been both deeply puzzled and impressed with the insight encapsulated in this notion from the point of view of moral philosophy. The puzzle arises from my discontent with the common but now fairly standard rendering of *li** as "principle." To forestall any misunderstanding, let me articulate as clearly as I can my dissatisfaction with this rendering. My difficulty is not with the translation as such, for obviously there is no proper equivalent term in English that can do the variety of jobs *li** does in Neo-Confucian philosophy. The term "principle" seems to come closest to *li** as a substantive. But when we take *li** in this way, we begin to wonder what kind of principle is at issue. Are we faced here with a sort of categorial principle immediately suggestive of an implicit philosophical system consisting of a body of statements that are mutually consistent *and* connected in a manner that can be clearly laid out? But if our answer is affirmative, will not the system appear deductive? This seems to be contrary to Neo-Confucianism, particularly in Wang's case. Furthermore, to construe *li** as a categorial notion implies that *li** is in some sense a classificatory notion, such that the invocation of *li**, in effect, would furnish us an instantiation of a category-in-use. Again, this suggestion appears to be completely alien to Chu Hsi—or, more important, to Wang. For Wang's moral philosophy, this suggestion is especially misleading because of his monistic tendency, which we shall consider later [4.9].

If the so-called principle is not categorial or classificatory, is it then a principle of factual description? Again, this interpretation is highly implausible for Wang, for he is not interested in mere factual description of an action or state of affairs. If it is a description, it is more an evaluative redescription than a straightforward factual description. The *li** of filial piety is quite unlike the *li** of a table, though it must be admitted that Wang shows no interest in the latter unless it is in some way related to the former and the like.[38] On the other hand, if in Wang's case we construe *li** as moral principles, a question immediately arises as to whether these so-called principles are objective or subjective, universal or relativistic. In pondering Wang's conception, I fail to arrive at any clear and satisfactory answers to these questions, though the rendering of *li** as principle is valuable in suggesting that *li** has a de jure or authoritative, and not merely a de facto, character; but many rules also have this character. There is a need, then, to locate more specifically the sort of "moral principles" that are distinct from nonmoral ones. Moreover, the notion of moral principles itself is problematic.[39] It is perhaps best to avoid, in particular, its association with different theories of moral justification. Although *li** is in some sense a justificatory notion, we must leave open for inquiry the nature of justification involved in the use of *li**. Deployment of a model derived from a theory of moral justification is, I believe, bound to mislead rather than throw light on the notion of *li**.

2.11   The problem in plausibly explicating *li** is to find some notion that is free from complicating and irrelevant implications for Wang's moral psychology. This task is greatly simplified if we can find a functionally equivalent notion in English. Since, for Wang, *li** is a fluid notion that admits of no precise definition, any functionally equivalent notion must carry more or less the same degree of indeterminacy. I shall assume that, for Wang, *li** is not ambiguous but an open-textured notion subject to specification in proper contexts of discourse. But instead of dealing directly with *li** as an isolated notion, I shall focus on a number of uses of *li** as it occurs in certain compound expressions in Wang's works. And in each of these cases I offer an interpretation which, I believe, is founded on textual evidence, independently plausible, and interesting for moral philosophy. The coherent thesis that emerges in my explication appears to offer a useful alternative to standard theories of moral justification. I leave for the future the development of this view as a contribution to moral epistemology. For the present, I should be content merely with the initial plausibility of the thesis.

   More fully, my procedure rests on Hsün Tzu's distinction between generic terms *(kung ming)* and specific terms *(pieh ming)*.[40] *Li** as a generic notion is subject to specification in contexts for which we have a substitution instance of either of the following schemata:

S1: "The *li** of *x*."
S2: "The *x* of *li**."

For example: "the *li** of filial piety" for S1 and "the significance of *li**" for S2. As we shall see, S1 is more appropriate for Confucian aretaic notions and S2 is more general in focusing on the significance of Confucian aretaic notions. Thus we may sometimes have to expand S2 into S2′—that is, "the *x* of the *li** of *y*," where *y* is a placeholder for aretaic notions and *x* is a placeholder for the significance of these aretaic notions. It must be observed that the distinction is not an absolute one, for S1 is necessary for explicating *li** as a generic term. I shall begin with *li** as a highest generic notion.[41] But a fuller understanding awaits our later treatment of Wang's conception of *li** in relation to moral reflection [3.5].

2.12 As a point of departure, I offer the notion of *reason* as functionally equivalent to *li**. The task consists in dealing with certain compound expressions in terms of "reason" construed as a reason-giving notion open to elaboration in articulate moral discourse. This proposal has a partial sanction in the modern Chinese notion of *li*-yu*, which can be rendered as "reason" or "ground." Reason-giving is an act of justification, but whether it takes the form of reasoning or the use of argument remains an open question. This conception of reasoning has no interest for Wang, however, and can play no useful role in our explication. Let us now take up a series of passages involving compound expressions and see how the functional equivalent of *li** can help us in our task. Consider first the following:

Passage H:
When the mind is free from the obscuration of selfish desires, it is the embodiment of *t'ien-li**, which requires not an iota added from the outside. When this mind is completely invested with

t'ien-li* and manifests *(fa)* itself in serving parents, there is filial piety. When it manifests itself in serving the ruler, there is loyalty. And when it manifests itself in dealing with friends or in governing the people, there are faithfulness and humanity *(jen)*.[42]

The expression *t'ien-li** also occurs in "to preserve [or abide by] *t'ien-li** and eliminate selfish desires," for which the passage is offered as an elucidation. If we construe *t'ien* as the totality of things in both the human and natural worlds, then the "*li** of *t'ien*" would be the *reason* that underlies such a totality. This reason is an ideal theme rather than an ideal norm. This ideal reason is therefore an expression of a perspective for dealing with all matters, which for Wang is a vision of the unity and harmony of all things. This vision is more commonly expressed by the notion of *jen* or *tao*, the significance of which cannot be exhausted with any claim to finality *(tao wu chung-ch'ung)*.[43] To possess *t'ien-li** is to be in a state of complete clarity of mind, intelligently discerning that the totality of things has the underlying ideal reason. The notion of *t'ien-li** is thus a generic notion of the ideal of the highest good *(chih-shan)* and not a specific notion referring to particular ideals that may be said to be expressed by such aretaic notions as filial piety or loyalty. Moreover, the ideal theme is not strictly a subject of argumentative discourse; for it is, according to Wang, a matter of personal realization.[44] When the mind abides by this condition of clarity or *t'ien-li**, it can also be said to be in a condition of mindfulness of the *li** of things to which our will is directed [2.3].

Given this condition as a point of departure *(t'ou nao)*, one can then inquire into the relevant facts. When the mind is completely invested with *t'ien-li** and devoid of selfish desires, it can then proceed to pay particular attention *(chiang-chiu)* to ways of manifesting the virtues appropriate to the subject and occasion of moral performance. In Wang's words:

If the mind is sincere in its filial piety of parents, then in the winter it will naturally think of the cold of parents and seek a way to provide warmth for them and in the summer it will naturally think of the heat of parents and seek a way to provide coolness for them. These are all offshoots of the mind that is sincere in its filial piety. Nevertheless, there must first be such a mind before there can be these offshoots.[45]

The relevant factual inquiry depends on *t'ien-li** as a basis. Such intellectual activities as thinking, inquiring, and discriminating are necessary, but they are subservient to the effort directed to the realization of the highest good.[46] They are not conducted for the sake of intellectual edification [2.1]. Focusing on abiding by *t'ien-li** as a state or condition, it is an exemplary moral achievement characteristic of sagehood. Only the sage can be in this condition continuously. But given Wang's Confucian faith in the ability of everyone to attain this state, sagehood can also be a goal of ordinary moral struggle [3.2].

At this juncture, one can properly inquire into the plausibility of construing *t'ien-li** as an ideal reason. Because it is a conception of the good life as a whole, an ideal theme can function as a reason in response to the question "Why, in general, does one engage in moral pursuit in particular circumstances?" Or as a response to the question "Why does one take the aretaic notions seriously as having an actuating import in one's moral life?" A moral agent can in this way appeal to *t'ien-li** as an ideal reason in justifying his active moral concern. But as an ideal reason, *t'ien-li** expresses not precepts but a mere perspective for action. It renders intelligible action as a constitutive feature of one's moral preoccupation. As a vision of moral excellence, it is also more fundamentally —as the metaphor of vision suggests—a way of seeing things as a relevant subject of morality in the broad sense. In a passionate tone, echoing Chang Tsai and Ch'eng Hao, Wang pronounces: "The great man considers Heaven, Earth, and myriad things as one body *(ti)*. He *sees (shih**)* the world *as* one family and the country *as* one person." In the language of *jen* (humanity), the great man also "forms one body" not only with a child, but also with birds and animals, plants, or even with tiles and stones."⁴⁷ *T'ien-li** may thus be said to express the ideal of *jen*, manifesting itself in the active Confucian's concern for the existence of things. It is an ideal capable of affective diffusion in the course of the commitive agent's encounter with the world of things. We may call this ideal a *Weltanshauung*; but as a moral vision it is "a basic orientation from which specific moral beliefs get their sense,"⁴⁸ that is, their significance or import. A vision or perspective for *seeing* things *as* possessing ideal import recalls its affinity with Wittgenstein's notion of aspect-seeing in our discussion of Wang's aesthetic analogy [1.6]. We may regard the present notion as an extension of Wittgenstein's notion of seeing-as for the purpose of focusing on the function of the ideal of *jen*, or *tao*, or *t'ien-li**. The ideal here is the reason or ground for using aretaic notions in general. Put differently, it is the reason of moral reasons. When the mind embodies *t'ien-li** and expresses itself in filial piety, for example, "there is the *li** of filial piety."⁴⁹

In light of the preceding discussion, *t'ien-li** is a generic *(kung ming)* rather than a specific notion of reason; moreover, it is the highest generic notion subject to specification in terms of the *li** of aretaic notions.⁵⁰ If my claim is acceptable, *t'ien-li** cannot function as a categorial notion, for its reference pertains to an ideal perspective that has no prescriptive import for the classification of moral actions or phenomena. Moreover, it has no explanatory function, for it is hardly intelligible to answer the question "Why does one perform such-and-such moral action?" by saying that "*t'ien-li** requires such-and-such moral action." The proper answer, however, can invoke one of the aretaic notions. Such an explanation can function at the same time as a justification. It is, moreover, our justificatory interest that generates the relevance of such an explanation. Just as we can invoke a second-order moral desire as a motive-explanation for moral achievement [2.6], we can also appeal to an aretaic notion as an explanation for an action in a specific context; but here the accent is placed on the context of a particular circumstance and not on the general second-order desire to do good or to comport with the ideal theme. The actual working of aretaic notions is, of course, grounded in the ideal; but this grounding relation is better understood in terms of the distinction and connection between the latent *(yin)* and the manifest *(hsien)* in sec. 1 of the *Doctrine of the Mean (Chung Yung)* and not in terms of the notion of subsumption in deductive inference. Thus *t'ien-li** cannot function as a premise in moral reasoning even if such a form of reasoning can be regarded as nondeductive, for no rules or precepts can be derived from it as an ideal theme. This point will become clearer as we consider another compound expression: *"tao-li."*

2.13 In explaining Mencius' saying that "holding the mean *(chung)* without allowing for special circumstances is like holding onto one particular thing," Wang points out that

> *Passage I:*
> The mean is nothing but *t'ien-li**; it is nothing but the Change. It changes according to the time. How can one hold it fast? One must have a sense of timing in determining what is the appropriate thing to do *(yin-shih chi-i)*. It is difficult to fix a pattern or action in advance. Later scholars insist on describing *tao-li** in their minute details leaving out nothing and prescribing a rigid pattern of action. This is the exact meaning of holding onto one particular thing.[51]

Apart from being a trenchant comment on Mencius' saying, the passage suggests that *t'ien-li** and *tao-li** are interchangeable expressions. However, *t'ien-li**, as it occurs in "abide by

t'ien-li*," expresses a state of possessing *tao* whereas in the
present occurrence it expresses the dynamic indeterminacy of
tao as an ideal theme. As we have previously noted, the significance of *tao*, while it can function as an ideal reason *(li*)*,
cannot be fixed in advance of actual encounter with particular situations [2.12]. We may thus regard *tao-li** as the *tao of
li**—that is, *tao* functioning as an ideal reason—but this reason-giving function cannot be stated as a set of rules or pre-
scriptions, for to do so is to hold onto a particular thing. The
point is not that rules must be formulated with exempting
clauses, but rather that rules themselves represent an arbitrary device for fixing the significance of the ideal theme. In
so doing it deprives the ideal of its continuing significance for
the course of human life. In Wang's vivid language, *"Tao-li**
has neither spatial restrictions nor physical form, and it cannot be pinned down to any particular. To seek it by confining
ourselves to literal meanings would be far off the mark."[52]

It cannot be denied that *tao-li** can be rendered as "moral
principles." But if such a rendering is to be free from misleading associations, it is perhaps best accompanied by an explanatory commentary. This construction presupposes that
the *tao* in *tao-li** is an adjective that implies an attribution of
the quality *tao* to *li** as principles.[53]

If I am correct in regarding *tao* as an ideal theme, the principles under discussion here would be ideal-embedded principles rather than deontic principles in the Kantian sense. If,
moreover, these so-called principles are formulated in accord
with a person's own understanding of the preceptive requirements of the aretaic notions, the *li** can properly be viewed as
principles for the person who is committed to them as action
guides. But these principles represent only the person's own
interpretation of what the aretaic notions mean for his conduct. They are best called "preceptive principles"—that is,
"first-personal precepts adopted by particular persons and dependent for their authority entirely upon such person's loyalty to them."[54] When an agent is sincerely and wholeheartedly

committed to *tao* as an ideal theme, there is no bar to his attempt at formulating precepts, via the aretaic notions, as policies of action to guide his conduct. But whether the aretaic notions have the same preceptive force for other agents is an open question. These precepts may have no relevance for other agents because of their differences in circumstance and understanding of the aretaic notions. An agent can, of course, publicly advocate his precepts, but advocacy is subject to critical consideration and acceptance by others; it is not a self-certifying authoritative pronouncement. For him to thrust his precepts upon others is an assertion of arrogance. And here we may say with Wang that "a great defect in life is pride. . . . Humility is the foundation of all virtues, while pride is the chief of all vices."[55] Besides, "the *tao* is public and belongs to the whole world, and the doctrine is also public and belongs to the whole world. They are not the private properties of Master Chu or even Confucius."[56] Principles as first-personal precepts are not universal. They are a personal articulation of the significance of aretaic notions that can at most have a *projective* function for other moral agents, and this is so because of the recognition by fellow agents that one is a paradigmatic individual.[57]

2.14   Apparently contrary to my explication of passage I, we find Wang saying that "it is because of *tao-li**∗** that there is relative importance."[58] This is a reply to a question concerning the consistency of his vision that "the great man and things form one body" with the *Great Learning*'s emphasis on "the relative importance among things." Wang then offers a rather lengthy discussion which involves another interesting compound expression: *t'iao-li**∗**. I shall postpone consideration of this expression [2.17] and concentrate here on Wang's elaboration. A partial quotation follows:

> *Passage J:*
> We love both plants and animals, and yet we can tolerate feeding

animals with plants. We love both animals and men and yet we can tolerate butchering animals to feed our parents, provide for religious sacrifices, and entertain guests. We love both parents and strangers. But suppose here are a small basket of rice and a platter of soup. With them one will survive and without them one will die. Since not both our parents and stranger can be saved by this meager food, we will prefer to save our parents instead of the stranger. This we can tolerate. We can tolerate all these because by *tao-li** these should be done. As to the relationship between ourselves and our parents there cannot be any distinction of this or that or of greater or lesser importance. For being humane to all people and feeling love for all comes from this affection toward parents. If in this relationship we can tolerate any relative importance, then anything can be tolerated.[59]

Let me first address Wang's statement that "it is because of *tao-li** that there is relative importance." This statement admits of two different interpretations. If we take it to mean that the *tao-li** itself contains a directive for a distinct order of values, this implies that *tao-li** is an axiological principle establishing a hierarchy of values. This, however, is plainly inconsistent with passage I. On the other hand, the statement can also, and more plausibly, be taken as pointing to *tao-li** as the basis of any conception of relative importance. This would mean that an ideal theme in the process of realization *may* call for comparative value judgments, particularly in situations where individuals confront moral dilemmas. In such situations, as in Wang's example of the competing demands for food from both one's parents and strangers, one must make a determinate judgment, however painful. Recall Mencius' remark that "a wise man knows everything, but he considers urgent only that which demands attention. A man of *jen* loves everyone, but he devotes himself to the close association with good and wise men. Even Yao and Shun did not use their wisdom on all things alike; this is because they put first things first."[60] Moral dilemmas are an experience of conflict between values in urgent or exigent situations. Here *tao* as *jen* or an ideal theme can guide the agent's cultivated sense of priority that gives rise to an occasional comparative value judgment.[61] This does not mean that *tao* itself embodies a normative hierarchy of values or rules for judgment, but it is quite compatible with the agent's making such a judgment in particular circumstances.

2.15   At this juncture, one may enter an objection: "Were there no such objective hierarchy, we would have to be content with taking value to rest on the questionable supposition that because men find something to be good, it is good."[62] This objection raises a most challenging problem for Confucian ethics. There appear to be two possible rejoinders. Developing a suggestion of Mencius, but not necessarily committing oneself to his doctrine of the innate goodness of human nature, one can say that "*jen* is man's proper abode, and *i* [rightness] is his proper path."[63] So long as the agent is earnest in his pursuit of *jen*, what is right is occasionally determined by circumstance. And in a situation of deep moral conflict the rightness of conduct may well be judged by a comparative ranking of competing goods. Ranking *x* as superior to *y* in one context does presuppose a scale of values, but since such a scale cannot be logically derived from the ideal of *jen*, it is possible that in another context *y* will hold the position of superiority. There are no comparative judgments required in advance of confrontation with particular cases. A comparative judgment is, as a practical judgment, a dictate of particular urgency and not an a priori principle for resolving problems. One's judgment, of course, is subject to challenge by fellow agents. And as a responsible agent, one must attempt to vindicate oneself against any charge of wrong conduct.[64] Relativity does infect comparative value judgments, but since these judgments are open to discussion, they need not be regarded simply as expressions of arbitrary personal preferences. Here the objectivity takes the form of interpersonal moral discourse and does not entail the necessity of assent to any a priori hierarchy of values.

This rejoinder will hardly be convincing or even intelligible unless we bring in a conception implicit in Wang's notion of *tao* as *jen*.[65] Returning to passage J, we observe that every comparative judgment of values involves some sacrifice or loss of value. This loss can be tolerated, not because of one's absolute and a priori determination of the value of a thing, but because of the inevitability of the painful judgment occasioned by an exigent situation. A comparative judgment is thus not universalizable. In light of *jen*, every existent thing qua existent has to be respected and cared for. It has an integrity of its own. When a comparative judgment has to be made, as in the choice between providing food for one's parents and providing for strangers, it is to be made with a profound feeling of regret. One can hardly be happy with such a loss of value, though one may be quite properly content with having done the right thing in the circumstance. We may call this "regret without repudiation" in contradistinction to "remorse without repudiation."[66] The regret is an expression of humane concern. Moreover, the regret, unlike the guilt-oriented remorse, has a forward-looking significance. For this moral feeling does remind the agent that a value lost on one occasion has to be *restored* if possible on other occasions. If this is not possible, one has to bear with heavy heart the experience of a great calamity. The sense of tragedy is not an outcome of moral shame or guilt but an acceptance of the inevitable happening one has brought about. A responsible acceptance points to the need for constant efforts at rectifying the loss of values, rather than passive acceptance of the unhappy consequences of one's action in an exigent situation.

It may be asked why Wang exempts parental affection from the judgment of relative importance. Toward the end of passage J, we find an echo of Confucius' view that "being humane *(jen)* to all people and feeling love for all comes from this affection toward parents."[67] This remark need not be taken as an affirmation of the absolute value of filial affection, which is rather an essential *precondition* for the active realization of *jen* in one's life. A commitment to *jen* as an ideal of diffusive affection must have a beginning in some immediate human habitat. It is in the family, the setting of one's growth and moral maturity, that a commitment to *jen* is a commitment to an extension of affectionate concern by enlarging the ambience of personal relationships. The family is a basic precondition for the child's moral development and for learning the complexity and dexterity of moral notions. In the incisive words of a recent moral philosopher:

> Conspicuously in the family the lives of persons are bound tightly by the love that persons have for each other, the joys and delights they take in each others' good fortunes and achievements, the admiration, emulation and even idealization of others by which efforts are encouraged and burdens are lightened.[68]

Wang would add that moral learning, nourishing one's mind, is like nourishing the roots of a tree: "If the tree is to grow, the many branches must be trimmed when it is young. . . . It is a task of creating something out of nothing."[69]

Instead of extending familial affection, one can easily be diverted from the ideal through the attraction of love for external things. Single-minded devotion to the ideal, however, does not imply blind endeavor [1.11]. And in the special case of parental affection, filiality does not call for uncritical obedience to parental wishes. In *Hsün Tzu*, it is forcefully stated that there are three cases of justifiable disobedience: when compliance with parental wishes will put them more in danger than in peace; when it will bring disgrace rather than honor to them, and disobedience in this case properly constitutes righteousness (*i*)₁; and when it compels one to behave like a dumb creature rather than a man of moral cultivation.[70] Which of these considerations is relevant depends on the context and one's view. Again, there is need of an occasional judgment that may yield the unwanted consequence of hurting one's affection for one's parents. In Hsün Tzu's succinct and telling phrase, one must "exercise one's sense of rightness in meeting with changing circumstances *(yi i pian-ying)*."[71] Given perseverance in self-cultivation, what more can be reasonably expected of a moral agent than a responsible plunge into uncertain consequences? The judgment here is, in effect, a gamble with an indeterminate future, betraying an experiment in the significance of a moral ideal. As Wang reminds his pupils, even "the sage does not value foreknowledge. He only knows the incipient activating force of things and handles it in accordance with the circumstance."[72]

2.16 The preceding discussion of *tao-li** and *t'ien-li** was actually the result of my meditation on the next compound expression: *i-li**. Thus my treatment of this notion will be relatively brief. I find two important passages for this notion:

> *Passage K:*
> *I-li** exist in no fixed place and are not exhaustible. Please do not think that, when you have gotten something from conversation with me, that is all there is to it. There will be no end if we talk for ten, twenty, or fifty more years.[73]

> *Passage L:*
> When a sage is born with knowledge, it means *i-li** only and not such things as the names and varieties of ceremonies and music. It is clear that such things as the names and varieties of ceremonies and music have nothing to do with the effort to become a sage. Since by a sage's being born with knowledge is meant his possession of *i-li** only, . . . and learning through hard work also means learning this *i-li** only.[74]

Note that *tao-li** could have been used in place of *i-li** without affecting the sense of passage K. Similarly, *t'ien-li** could

have been used for *i-li** in passage J. Since the terms are interchangeable, the preceding discussion [2.12–2.13] suffices for
the treatment of these passages. Only one distinction requires
a reminder: While *t'ien-li** and *i-li**, when they are said to be
preserved or possessed, express a condition of sagely attainment or moral endeavor aiming at the realization of *tao* or
jen, *tao-li** directs attention to the dynamic indeterminacy of
tao or *jen* as an ideal theme. The classical Confucian idiom of
chih-shan ("highest good") could well replace *t'ien-li** and
*i-li**, but the notion of *li** in the latter term brings out
more perspicuously the justificatory force of the Confucian
vision.[75]

Nevertheless, *i-li** is worthy of independent exploration,
particularly in relation to the aretaic notions. We can regard
*i-li** as a conjunction of two substantives which, for Wang, refers to noncontingently connected aspects of the moral mind.
This interpretation is clearly suggested in the following passage:

Passage M:
What one calls *li** in an event or object *(wu)*, *i* in adapting ourselves towards it, and good *(shan)* in nature, are differently desig-
nated on account of things to which they refer, but in reality are
all manifestations of my mind *(hsin)*. When the mind regards
events and objects purely from the viewpoint of *li** and without
any admixture of falsity, there is good. This is not fixed in events
and objects, and can be sought for in a definite place. *I* means to
adapt oneself properly to objects: it refers to my mind having
done what is appropriate. For *i* is not an external object, which
one can seize and take over.[76]

It is interesting to observe that *i* in one basic sense is "rightness" or "appropriateness." When it is conjoined with *li** construed as reason, the compound expression could be rendered
as the rightness or appropriateness of reason to an occurrent

situation. It is difficult not to yield to the temptation of intro-
ducing the Aristotelian notion of right reason. Wang could
well endorse the thesis that "virtue or excellence is not only a
characteristic which is guided by right reason, but also a
characteristic which is united with right reason; and right
reason in moral matters is practical wisdom."[77] Of course, we
find in Wang no extensive discussion of i that would suggest
Aristotle's complex and detailed conception of practical wisdom. Moreover, it would be farfetched to ascribe any doctrine of practical syllogism to Wang. But insofar as both
philosophers lay stress on the appropriateness of reason to
particular circumstances, both have insight into an aspect of
prospective moral knowledge.

More clearly for i-li*, we may use schema S2—that is, "the
i of li*"—and explain it as "the appropriateness of li* (reason)
to an occurrent circumstance" [2.11]. However, i can also be
rendered as "meaning." And since both passages K and L rule
out any concern with the semantics of linguistic expressions,
our only recourse is to construe it as a pragmatic term functionally equivalent to "significance" or "import." And when
we deploy schema S2 for aretaic notions, then the "i of the li*
of aretaic notions" could be interpreted as "the significance of
the li* of aretaic notions to actual circumstances." This is
quite in consonance with the basic sense of i as appropriateness. For the li* of aretaic notions are those notions which
function as *reasons for action*. This is the li* or justificatory
force of aretaic notions as appropriate in the context of particular circumstances or existing situations affecting a moral
agent. I is thus a context-variable notion.

In other words, aretaic notions cannot function as reasons for action apart from their appropriateness to particular
situations. Herein lies their significance or "cash value." Of
course, they can also be used for the ascription of moral qualities to the agent [1.7]. But in view of changing circum-

stances, their ascriptive uses have only the status of "credit value," pending the display of moral qualities in actual performance. The *li** of aretaic notions as reasons for action are not amenable to theoretical systematization. We do not have here a theory of practical reasoning, for Wang's interest concerns prospective moral knowledge rather than the theoretical status of the aretaic notions [1.3]. If one demands a criterion for distinguishing good from bad reasons for action, one is bound to be disappointed. Perhaps on behalf of Wang, one could claim that the question is unintelligible with respect to prospective moral knowledge. This reply is obviously not helpful to the epistemological query. But for moral psychology, the notion of *i* does bring out an important feature of the exercise of moral agency. Like its homophone *yi* ("will"), *i* is a mediating factor between prospective moral knowledge and action or retrospective moral knowledge [2.3], with special reference to the pragmatic significance of the aretaic notions. An engaging question remains, however. When *li** is in fact present in an occurrent situation, and one acts accordingly with a sense of appropriateness, what can be said about the character of one's retrospective knowledge? For a possible answer, let us reflect on Wang's use of another compound expression: *t'iao-li**.

2.17   In one terse statement, Wang explains *li** in terms of *t'iao-li**.[78] *T'iao-li** refers to pattern or order. The etymology of *li** does suggest this reading—that is, the polishing of gems according to their veins.[79] In this sense, *li** may be said to embody a conception, to borrow Moore's term, of organic unity.[80] As Needham points out, "there is 'law' implicit in it, but this law is the law to which parts of a whole have to conform by virtue of their very existence as parts of a whole."[81] We have, in other words, a conception of a gestalt rather than an aggregative order. If the mind is in a state of complete clarity or abides by *t'ien-li** without obscuration by selfish desires, Wang believes that it has this knowledge of *li** as a gestalt or organic unity. Wang explains:

Passage N:
For instance, we see the heaven in front of us. It is [a] bright and clear heaven. If we see heaven outside the house, it is the same bright and clear heaven. Only because it is obscured by these many walls of the building do we not see heaven in its entirety. If we tear down the walls, we will only see one heaven. We should not say that what is in front of us is the bright and clear heaven but what is outside the house is not. From this we can comprehend how the knowledge of a part is [in some sense] the same as the knowledge of a whole, and the knowledge of the whole is [in some sense] the same as knowledge of a part. All is one original substance *(pen-ti).*[82]

The knowledge here appears to be retrospective moral knowledge. It is the knowledge of moral achievement. This point is compatible with and complementary to our discussion of *i-li** [2.16]. When the agent succeeds in acting with a sense of appropriateness guided by his understanding of the actuating import of an aretaic notion, his action has thus an orderly appearance. This orderliness is what *emerges* when his action is in complete accord with what the situation required. *Li** as orderliness is thus a supervenient and not a constitutive property of action. It is, to borrow Ross's term, a *toti-resultant attribute*—that is, "one which belongs to an act in virtue of its whole nature and nothing less than this."[83]

With respect to things which are not acts, *li** may also be said to be *in* them, as for example in passage M, but saying this offers us no information concerning the nature of things as they are in themselves. Since, for Wang, a thing *(wu)* is that to which the *yi* (will or intention) is directed [2.3], a thing, in this sense, is more an objective of the moral will than an object existing in its own right. Thus in commenting on Ch'eng I's remark that "what is inherent in a thing is *li**," Wang points out that "the word 'mind' should be added to the saying to mean that when the mind is engaged in a thing, there is *li**. For example, when the mind is engaged in serving one's father, there is the *li** of filial piety, and when the mind is engaged in serving the ruler, there is the *li** of loyalty, and so forth."[84] This remark suggests that without moral concern expressed in will or intention, objects in themselves command no intrinsic interest for us as moral agents. When an object becomes an objective in our activity, whether in inquiry or in discrimination [2.1], it thus acquires a quality of moral concern [2.2]. In serving one's parents, for instance, one has to think of provision for their comfort in summer and in winter because one has a moral point of departure [2.12]. When things thus acquire a quality owing to our moral concern and varying intellectual activities, their quality is a consequence of the things' possession of certain describable properties.[85]

It is instructive in considering *li** as orderliness to observe that Wang explicitly connects it with its homophone *li* ("propriety"):

> The word *li* [propriety] has the same purport as the word *li**. When *li** becomes manifest and can be seen, we call them patterns *(wen)* and when patterns are hidden and obstruse and cannot be seen we call them *li**. They are only one thing. Restraining oneself with the rules of propriety is only to enable the mind to be completely invested with *t'ien-li**. In order for the mind to be so invested with *t'ien-li**, one must direct one's effort to wherever *li** is manifested.[86]

This remark suggests that both *li* and *li** have the same purport in indicating order. The former typically is an explicit form or pattern *(wen)* of the latter.[87] In this sense, *li* is the manifest order of *li**, and *li** the hidden order *li*. But since

li* as in *t'ien-li** is an ideal reason for aretaic notions which
can function as reasons for action [2.16], *li* can also be regarded as an actual achievement of an ideally reasonable order. In the case of an individual performance, it is a visible
form *(wen)* of an achievement of orderliness that results from
compliance with *li* as a body of ritual rules, but with an implicit understanding that the form serves as a sign of the presence of a moral virtue.[88] *Li* as an aretaic notion can also be
properly construed as referring to the quality of a community
—that is, as an achieved quality that pervades the varying
contexts of human relationships, a quality of social harmony.
In this sense, *li* is an ideal-embedded aretaic notion. Not all
social orders are thus morally acceptable. *Li* as an achievement belongs to the realm of *li**, that is, the realm of reasons
for action or the realm of the reasonable order in a moral
community. It is a temporary realization of an ideal order—
an occasional moral achievement that can be an object of retrospective moral knowledge.

2.18   Prospectively, *li** as orderliness appears as a moral task. Prospective knowledge may thus be said to be the indwelling
spirit *(ling ch'u)* of *li** [2.9]. Hence knowledge and action are,
in this light, "really two words describing the same effort."[89]
Graham's examination of *li** in Ch'eng Hao and Ch'eng I directs our attention to the use of *li** as "accounting not for the
properties of a thing but for a task it must perform to occupy
its place in the natural order."[90] Viewed in light of *t'ien-li**,
then, *tao* or *jen*—as an ideal theme, the "natural order" for
Wang—is an ideal-embedded order, that is, an order achieved
when one becomes a great personage or a sage who "forms
one body" with all things [2.12]. For ordinary agents, *li** as
order is a task to be accomplished, but the achieved order is
something that can be envisaged in one's imagination relative
to a current situation. This envisagement does not amount
to a prediction or predetermination of the nature of moral

achievement.[91] The description of the order achieved depends on one's actual experience, not on a correspondence of the imaginative picture to actual states of affairs. It is important to inquire into the nature of the moral reflection involved in *li** as a moral task [3.5]. But before we pursue this challenging topic, let us recapitulate the results of our discussion of *li** in relation to Wang's doctrine of the unity of knowledge and action.

2.19 Our discussion of *li** has been prompted by a desire to give a plausible explication of Wang's compendious remark (passage G) on the unity of knowledge and action: "Knowledge is the intelligent locus *(ling-ch'u)* of *li**" [2.9]. In order to understand this notion of *li**, I have construed it as basically a generic notion subject to specification in terms of the uses of aretaic notions. As a functional equivalent for *li**, I offered the notion of reason and proceeded to examine a number of compound expressions: *t'ien-li**, *tao-li**, *i-li**, and *t'iao-li**. *T'ien-li** is *tao* or the ideal of *jen* functioning as a reason for aretaic notions, which are in turn reasons for actions. *Tao-li**, while interchangeable with *t'ien-li*, which for the most part refers to the clarity of mind involved in the attainment of *tao*, focuses instead on the dynamic indeterminacy of *tao* or *jen* as an ideal theme. *I-li** more specifically points to the relevance of aretaic notions in particular situations. In retrospect, when the agent succeeds in acting in consonance with a situation at hand, he may be said to have attained *t'iao-li**. *T'iao-li** is thus an occasional achievement of a temporal practical order. At the same time, viewed prospectively, *t'iao-li** is a moral task. In effect, my proposal for rendering *li** as reason is really a proposal for rendering *li** as *reasonableness*. Reasonableness is more a characteristic of moral agents than a characteristic of moral knowledge viewed solely in terms of its intellectual or cognitive content apart from its actuating import [4.12–4.19]. Not surprisingly, reasonableness, unlike rationality, admits of no formulation in terms of criteria. For passage G, "knowledge is the intelligent locus of *li**," we may now say that "knowledge, retrospectively, is the indwelling spirit of reasonableness" [2.9].

Although reasonableness cannot be intelligibly conceived in terms of canons, it can nevertheless guide the agent in moral reflection. In this light, given the acceptability of my explication of Wang's doctrine, we can properly say that the unity of knowledge and action as a doctrine concerning the transition from prospective to retrospective moral knowledge [1.12] involves not only *yi*, playing a complex mediating role as volition, intention, motive, and second-order moral desire [2.7], but also *li** as reasonableness in the successful exercise of moral agency. The four compendious remarks which I have labeled D, E, F, and G may thus be regarded as conceptual reminders of the complexity of the successful exercise of moral agency [1.10, 2.2, 2.9].

3 Confucian Vision, Commitment, and Moral Reflection

3.1   In the preceding explication of Wang's doctrine of the unity of moral knowledge and action, we found it difficult to give a full account of that doctrine without invoking the Confucian vision of the harmony of man and nature—an ideal of human excellence alternatively termed *tao* or *jen* ("humanity"). We have seen that this vision is best taken as an ideal theme or a perspective for orientation rather than as an ideal norm that can be explicated in terms of criteria for moral conduct [2.12]. This recourse to the notion of *tao* and *jen* quite naturally raises the question of the coherence of the Confucian vision. Unless one can render intelligible the coherence of this vision, Wang's moral psychology, though interesting and plausible in its own right, appears to be set on a shaky foundation. Moreover, it remains unclear how a commitive Confucian agent is to pursue this task without specific guidance.

    I suggest that a profitable way to deal with this question is to view the Confucian *tao* or *jen* as a coherent notion of the harmony of man and nature in the *nonsystematic* sense. Although for Wang, as for his Neo-Confucian predecessors, the vision is also a comprehensive conception that embraces all things in the universe, we find no systematic ontology with a categorial scheme for the explanation and classification of existent entities and their relation to one another. In particular, we are offered nothing akin to the chain of beings or a hierarchy of entities in superordinate or subordinate relations. Especially in Wang's case, this notion, as we have seen, is contrary to his doctrine of the unity of moral knowledge and action. *Li**, of course, is said to be inherent in all things, but in moral contexts this amounts to saying no more than that things are objects of appropriate moral concern [2.17]. I do not deny that *li** can properly be regarded as a quasi-metaphysical notion—that is, a root metaphor for developing a categorial system.[1] Ch'eng I's famous saying, "*Li** is one, but its manifestations are many," does appear to be a promising root metaphor.[2] It expresses a concern with the problems of the one and the many, of being and becoming, and is thus reminiscent of a basic topic in Western metaphysics. Further, as suggestive of a notion of organic unity, *li** can serve as a basis for developing metaphysical systems. Since our interest lies in Confucian moral psychology, we must leave this inquiry for others who are more concerned with Confucian metaphysics.

When we focus on the Confucian vision as a moral vision, we find that its coherence and import do not depend on having a systematic ontology. Seen in light of the Confucian concern with moral theory as a task of practical rather than intellectual understanding, the absence of a categorial scheme does not affect the vision's coherence. From this point of view, *tao* or *jen* is best construed as a coherent *ideal attitude* or a perspective for organizing or unifying the diverse and conflicting elements of moral experience. It is important to note that in the *Doctrine of the Mean*, the notion of harmony is explained in psychological terms. "Before feelings of pleasure, anger, sorrow, and joy are aroused it is called equilibrium *(chung)* [or centrality or the mean]. When these feelings are aroused and each and all attain due measure and degree, it is called harmony *(ho)*."[3] The notion of *ho* or harmony is expressive of an ideal attitude toward one's feelings—ultimately, a way of looking at all things inclusive of human affairs and natural events. The comprehensive attitude at issue does not necessarily involve a systematic theory or a clear and precise idea that unveils the constitutive elements of thought and action. In short, the ideal attitude has a significance quite apart from the ability of the agent to articulate its nature and import in terms of a coherent set of propositions.

To adopt *tao* or *jen* as a governing ideal of one's life does not imply a determinate conception of the ideal to be realized. It is to adopt an attitude and to resolve, with one's mind and heart *(hsin)*, to look at things and events in a way in which they can become constituents in a harmonious unity that is not specified in advance of man's confrontation with changes in the natural world. To adopt this ideal attitude is to see human life in its morally excellent form, as possessing a coherence in which apparently conflicting elements are viewed as eligible elements of an achievable harmonious order. The presence of conflicting elements in experience is a fact to be acknowledged. This acknowledgment brings with it the necessity of reconciliation. As Cheng rightly points out, the adoption of the ideal of harmony, together with the view of opposites as complements, paves the way toward a dialectics of harmonization in Chinese philosophy.[4] Since the desired coherence of the moral order is not spelled out a priori, the harmonization of conflicting elements in experience is essentially a *creative* endeavor on the part of both the Confucian moral thinker and agent. The ideal of harmony is a notion of the dynamic interplay of man and nature. The discordant notes in experience set a *challenge* to man's efforts to actualize his vision of excellence. In terms of this vision the world of man and nature is not a static order with implications to be discerned by a process of logical inference. Consequently, a commitment to the Confucian vision carries a great burden, a creative burden calling for persevering sincerity *(cheng)* and seriousness *(ching)*. As Wang incisively observes, moral learning, the learning it takes to become a sage, is a creative process; it is "the task of creating something from nothing."[5]

Sagehood *(sheng)*, in the light of *tao* or *jen* as an ideal theme, can be attained by ordinary agents in varying degrees and circumstances of their lives. Except perhaps for a few individuals, attainment of sagehood does not appear to be an enduring state, for the harmony experienced is something that occurs at a particular moment in time and place. Such an experience cannot by itself foreclose the possibility of future issues or problems. The *tao* as an ideal attitude has thus a continuing relevance throughout the course of the commitive agent's life [2.13]. It may be noted, however, that a particular experience of harmony is not without its charm and significance. For typically such an experience gives rise to a sense of satisfaction indicative of a supervenient quality of moral achievement. In the manner of Aristotle, we may say that it is a quality of pleasure that "completes an activity not as a characteristic completes an activity, but as a completeness that superimposes itself upon it, like the bloom of youth in those who are in their prime."[6] As a style of moral achievement, such a sense of completion of one's own being is bound to differ from one agent to another, being representative of the varying ways in which a common vision is realized in individual styles of life. In this manner, two different agents may share the same vision and yet experience its import differently. And in different ways the styles of achievement increase the confidence of the commitive agents in search of future experiences of harmony.

Thus far we have focused on *ho* or harmony in the *Doctrine of the Mean*. The notion of *chung* ("equilibrium, mean, or centrality") appears to be another aspect of that Confucian classic. The two words, *chung* and *ho*, together may be regarded as the ideal of central harmony. *Chung*, or equilibrium, is said to be the state of mind prior to the arousal of emotions; the term is suggestive of a state of calmness, unperturbed by emotions. We have here a distinction without a dichotomy. As Wang points out, equilibrium *(chung)* and harmony *(ho)* are not contrasting states.[7] The distinction is more plausibly a distinction of two complementary mental states in the experience of *tao*. When emotions are aroused and expressed in concord *(ho)*, one naturally experiences a state of equilibrium. Equilibrium is here a state of consummatory quiescence attendant upon the successful effort at harmonizing one's emotions as well as thoughts and actions—an object of retrospective moral knowledge. Like the experience of harmony, such a state is bound to be transient. As Wang puts it, "unless we are sound asleep or dead like dry wood or dead ashes," we cannot avoid having thoughts.[8] To be alive is to engage in thought and action concerning one's feelings and desires; and to live in the light of *tao* or *jen* is to make it a paramount perspective in dealing with the conflicting elements of human life in the midst of changes in the natural world. The coherence of the Confucian *tao* thus provides only a point of orientation for meeting moral problems—not through specific rules of conduct but by way of a challenge to the agent to constitute the content and import of his commitment. Ultimately, the import of *tao* is a matter of personal realization.

3.2   In light of a commitment to *jen*, the problem of moral agency is seen by Wang to be a problem of becoming a sage. The task, as we have seen, has less to do with the acquisition of factual knowledge. Rather, it is a problem of constituting by way of thought and action the content and import of the vision of the harmony of man and nature [2.16]. From this viewpoint, the task of sagehood calls for no effort to develop effective strategies or instruments. Instead it calls for the cultivation of a personal character or quality of mind capable of realizing the ideal of harmony. The agent receives initial guidance from the moral tradition. The aretaic notions have an entrenched conventional content that provides guidance for moral learning and performance. Further, the Confucian classics have an important role to play, for they provide the basic source for interpreting the continuing relevance and criticism of current moral conventions. When Wang deals with these classics (such as the *Great Learning*), he is primarily interested in what he regards as insights implicit in them rather than textual exegesis, which for him represents nothing but fragmented moral learning [2.17]. In Kierkegaardian language, Wang is not an "objective thinker" concerned with the elaboration of an ethical theory that can serve as a rational foundation for morality; he is a *committed* thinker interested in the "subjective appropriation" of classical Confucian ideas.[9] The task of a moral thinker is also that of a moral agent. For Wang, it is largely a question of "how can a person become a Confucian moral agent?" (that is, a man of *jen*)—a question somewhat parallel to Kierkegaard's "how can one become a Christian?" It is a question concerning a personal transformation through the Confucian vision. It is a question of self-understanding and self-transformation.

3.3   Wang's doctrine of the unity of moral knowledge and action can thus be regarded as an incisive articulation of the nature of the Confucian commitment to *tao* or *jen* as an ideal theme. By focusing on the components of volitional, intentional, and intellectual acts in moral achievement, he has provided us with an elementary, though admittedly sketchy, anatomy of moral commitment. One intellectual activity at the service of our moral will deserves special attention. In approving of inquiry as a proper way of dispelling doubt [2.1], Wang in effect endorses the attitude of doubt as appropriate to one's effort to carry out a commitment to *jen* as an ideal theme. If retrospective moral knowledge is a condition of clarity of mind [2.9], this condition must emerge from stages of struggle with unclarity vis-à-vis the cognitive content encapsulated in the Confucian aretaic notions.

Doubt and clarity, from the prospective point of view, are thus compatible states of mind. If this point is granted, then when a person commits himself to *jen* he is also committed to the task of clarifying what *jen* means in his way of life. Unless the agent experiences doubt in the process of clarification, he may be too attached to his own congenial ideas and the conventions learned during his moral upbringing, thereby depriving himself of the possibility of a wider view and consideration of what actual situations mean in light of his ideal theme. Moreover, a sincere agent may at times, in the course of his moral life, experience doubt concerning the significance of his understanding of the ideal theme as offering a perdurable vision.

The possibility of such an experience can perhaps be appreciated if we distinguish between an actual and an ideal self. The commitment to an ideal theme is a commitment to a meaningful connection between the actual and the ideal self. Sincere doubt can occur in this way when the significance of an ideal theme is reconsidered in light of one's changing needs and desires. And these needs and desires are not necessarily selfish, though they are self-regarding demands that may be deemed reasonable, particularly in light of changing circumstances that affect one's moral efforts at continuing self-cultivation. Doubt points to the capacity of the reasonable agent to *reflect* upon what his ideal means as a continuing concern with living. Whether or not such a reflection will result in a change of heart is a question only the agent can answer. But if a commitment precludes reflective reconsideration, it cannot be viewed as a reasonable commitment. If this is so, reflection on the actuating import of an ideal theme is an integral component of the commitment.

3.4　　A commitment to *jen* has thus a dynamic character. A reasonable agent with a sense of *i* or rightness [2.16] will transform his initial understanding of the cognitive content of aretaic notions into something quite different when reflecting upon his moral performance. Although Wang seems to neglect this aspect, consistent with his emplasis on *i*, he could have paid heed to Chu Hsi's saying: "When one knows something but has not yet acted upon it, his knowledge is still shallow. After he has experienced it, his knowledge will be increasingly clear, and its character will be different from what it was before."[10] A commitment to *jen* as an ideal theme thereby carries both a liability and a challenge. The liability consists in being faithful to what one understands to be required by an aretaic notion in an occurrent situation. The dynamic character of the commitment lies in the manner in which prospective moral knowledge is transformed by the course of doing and, reciprocally, in the manner in which retrospective knowledge of an action, in turn, is transformed when it acquires the character of prospective knowledge in future situations. An experience of successful doing, unless it remains a mere condition of quiescence, has a *projective* significance for future endeavors. This significance is suggested in Wang's insistence that *tao* cannot be exhausted in determinate formulas for action [2.13]. If a successful course of moral endeavor in a particular setting terminates in a state of inactivity, for the person to resume his activity this state of affairs, as it were, must project a horizon for future accomplishment. In this sense, moral experience has a transcendent character— that is, it has a significance beyond the present situation. Moral being is moral becoming in action, mediated by thinking in concrete loci.

Being moral, for a reflective Confucian, consists in knowing and acting in ways which both interact and affect the nature of each. In abstraction from occurrent situations, retrospective moral knowledge has close affinity with the idea of genuine knowledge as maker's knowledge, "which covers also the notion of doer's knowledge." In this conception, "no distinction between *poesis* and *praxis* is intended." It is the idea "that we can obtain and possess certain especially valuable kinds of *theoretical* knowledge only of what we ourselves have brought about, are bringing about, or can bring about. It thus emphasizes certain theoretical uses of practical reason."[11]

But retrospective moral knowledge is not strictly maker's or doer's knowledge in the sense that the moral agent produces a specially valuable kind of moral knowledge. The practical knowledge possessed by the agent, not as something learned but as something he can claim to have achieved after the deed, is not, after all, something that he has literally made or produced. For unlike the artist, his actions are only intelligible in light of an established moral tradition embedded in aretaic notions. Compared to an artist, he has much less freedom to explore the possibility of carrying out his moral will or intention; moreover, his action is markedly limited by the context of a particular circumstance. The moral agent cannot produce new forms of action, though, like an artist, he can display a new style in the unique manner in which he deals with his moral tradition, by way, say, of *reconstituting* the import of a tradition—that is, by investing it with an import received from an ideal theme. Even in the case of critical acceptance of a tradition, moral achievement can display only, to use Pepper's terms, intrusive and not emergent novelties, though its experiential character is not subject to a conventional description.[12]

In the case of prospective knowledge as one kind of intentional knowledge, the situation of the moral agent committed to an ideal theme is much like that of the artist, in that neither kind of knowledge is tied to verbal description. As Hampshire points out:

I may know quite clearly what I am going to do in some future contingency, and my intention may be fixed and firm, although I would not be able to say, to put into words, exactly what I am to do, if I were asked. For example, an actor may be *entirely* clear in his own mind about how he is going to play a particular scene, even though, if you asked him to tell you how he is going to do it, he could only say—"Like this"—and then proceed to play it.[13]

Such prospective knowledge has no intrinsic epistemic significance unless it is couched in retrospective form—that is, when the agent has successfully carried out his intention in a current situation. And when it does, it is hardly distinguishable from retrospective moral knowledge. But prospective knowledge of an ideal theme is also a groping for clarification of the significance of an ideal theme. The intention formed as a response to a current case represents one articulation of the significance of an ideal theme. Such an articulation cannot be said to exhaust the meaning of *tao* or *jen* [2.19]. A commitment to an ideal theme is therefore preeminently a commitment to moral creativity.

Although retrospective moral knowledge is amenable to descriptive statement, this knowledge is not universal, for it differs in accordance with different agents' experiences of moral achievement. Just as we have no theory of ideal themes, we have no theory of creative moral agency and its products. Perhaps this is the insight in Wang's recurrent insistence on personal experience [1.8]. Of course, the moral achievements of different persons may be compared, particularly with respect to their freedom from yielding to the temptations of selfish desires. Sagehood, for Wang, is "comparable to pure gold which attains its purity because its golden quality is perfect and is no longer mixed with copper or lead. . . . However, the abilities of sages differ in degree, just as several pieces of gold differ in weight." Nevertheless, they are all called sages. "For to be pure gold depends not on quantity but on perfection in quality, and to be a sage depends not on ability or effort but only on having completely embodied *t'ien-li**"[14]—that is, being in a state of realization of the highest good [2.12]. One can write an autobiography or a biography of individual moral achievement, but one cannot generalize it into a universal account of moral achievement. This is the reason why no agent, insofar as he is aware of his creative burden, can imitate another. Quite in the spirit of Wang, we may say with the Neo-Taoist Kuo Hsiang:

> Those who imitate the sages imitate what they have already done. But what they have done is something already gone and therefore cannot meet the changes (of the present). Why then should we respect and cling to it? If we cling to the crystallized achievements (of the past) as a means for dealing with the amorphous (present), then the crystallized (past) acts as an obstruction to the amorphous (present).[15]

It is a logical corollary of this conception of moral creativity that moral achievement is an individual affair. An incisive biography of a moral agent may *exhibit* the concrete possibility of realizing an ideal theme; it does not exemplify a logical instantiation of the ideal. The ideal theme has no logical instances. It has variations on a theme, as in musical compositions, but these variations are not instances of an application of a rule or moral principle. In this realm of polymorphous achievements, one can perhaps discern a thread but no common logic.

3.5 Apart from inquiry as a way of dispelling doubt [3.3], one may ask what other activity is involved in moral reflection in occurrent situations. And is this activity, particularly in relation to *li** as a moral task [2.18], a quest for the organic unity of retrospective moral knowledge? Self-cultivation, with self-mastery in the discipline of the agent's feelings and desires, can help meet changing circumstances; but this is not a sufficient condition for moral achievement. At the heart of the moral life dedicated to the realization of the ideal theme of *jen*, the activity of thinking in terms of *li* * must aim at a harmonious integration of an agent's inner states and outward events. This form of thinking does not require calculation of the consequences of actions except insofar as they are considered as parts of the *jen*-achievement. Nor does the thinking require a set of ready-made recipes or a hierarchy of values to be applied in different circumstances [2.15]. Moral thinking is a sort of mind-in-action that is essentially a response to a concrete situation. For moral thinking to be effectively exercised, the Confucian agent must cultivate a mind responsive to every change that may occur in his life. An appropriate answer to a problematic situation depends primarily on thinking in a particular setting. Wang offers us no explicit view on this form of moral thinking, but we can perhaps throw some light on it by elaborating the notion of "reflection on things at hand" *(chin-ssu)*.[16] This notion appears implicit in Wang's comparison of the sage's mind to a clear mirror:

Passage O:
Since it is all clarity, it responds to all stimuli as they come and reflects everything. There is no such case as a previous image still remaining in the present reflection or yet-to-be-reflected image already existing there. . . . [The] sage does a thing when the time comes. . . . The study of changing conditions and events is to be done at the time of response.[17]

If we take this mirror metaphor seriously, it suggests two different features of moral reflection. In the first place, the moral mind-in-action, just like a clear mirror, reflects in the sense of receiving impressions of objects without pronouncing judgment. In the second place, the mind-in-action engages in reflection in the sense of thinking about what ought to be done. The first sense of reflection focuses on the receptive or passive capacity of the mind. This state of readiness, however, is a prelude to reflection in the second sense—that is, thinking at a particular time and place with respect to the appropriate course of action. Moral reflection proper pertains to this thinking in an occurrent situation.

Since the sage perfectly embodies *tao* or *jen*, his moral reflection and response can hardly be distinguished. Thus he spontaneously responds to "all things as they come." This spontaneous response is natural in the sense that it is unmediated by judgment. The sage, representing the ideal case of the moral life, may be said to have no mind or feelings, since his mind embodies the *tao*. He engages in no appraisal. But for ordinary agents, reflection on "changing conditions and events" is indispensable. Moral reflection here is essentially an act of appraisal. What the agent ought to do finally depends on his judgment of the case at issue. In the normal course of human life, the judgment is made without much effort since the ordinary agent is equipped with moral learning —that is, a conventional set of rules and precepts. But whether or not the established rules in one's moral community are relevant to a case at hand is a question to be decided after "study of the changing conditions or events." In other words, the decision rests on a judgment of the relevance of rules to a particular circumstance. When the situation is an unfamiliar or exigent case, moral reflection requires some effort in appreciating the situation before judgment. In either normal or exigent cases, appreciating the situation is an essential component of moral reflection. Put another way, moral judgment is a judgment mediated by an appreciation of the situation. Wang's stress on "the time of response" focuses on the necessity of making an *independent* judgment adequate to the case at hand. In the language of *li**, the *li** of each case cannot be determined a priori. In this view, moral reflection is clearly not a deductive process. Nor is it an inductive generalization from particular cases. Even if conventional rules are deemed relevant, the relevance at issue is an outcome of the agent's appraisal. One may, of course, raise the question of justification of moral judgments. This question, however, goes beyond the scope of the present essay.

As a mind-in-action, moral reflection is a form of mindfulness. It is a selective attention to the distinctive features of the situation in terms of the agent's sense of importance.[18] The appreciation of an occurrent situation thus presupposes an evaluative judgment. This sense of importance has been emphasized by Wang [2.15]. Since moral reflection is directed to *li** as an organic unity, it is also mindful of the gestalt of the situation. Following Matson, we may say that it is an activity of *apperception*. That is, the distinctive features of the organic whole are "not only perceived, but are united and assimilated to a mass of ideas already possessed, and so comprehended and interpreted."[19] In terms of a commitment to *jen*, thinking in terms of *li** is principally an apperception based on a *moral* interest. The apperceived whole is in part a construction of the agent in abstraction from his total environment. The total environment may be objectively described, but at issue is a question of acting, a matter of weighing the right response to an occurrent situation. Relevance of the situational features is determined by *jen* or moral interest, not by an exhaustive survey or factual inquiry. The moral interest is concerned not with all facts of the case but only with those facts that are relevant to the realization of *jen* [2.1]. Since moral apperception contains an interpretive element, different agents may constitute in different ways the content and import of *jen*. As an overarching ideal theme, *jen* can be developed in various ways without losing its action-guiding function.

3.6   Moral reflection, since it involves an appreciation of the situation, obviously carries a liability of error. Nevertheless, the judgment of importance is a *constitutive* feature of the situation. And when the judgment is regarded as paradigmatic by fellow agents, the judgment, in place of a rule, can serve as a guide to others' moral apperception. The notion of a moral situation is not a mere descriptive concept. For the Confucian agent, *jen* implies a moral relation between human beings. He can agree with Kovesi that "situations are not out there in the world, existing independently of us, so that human beings could just step in and out of them. . . . To be in a situation is to be related to other human beings in a certain way."[20] In terms of *li**, moral situations pertain to the shared status of human beings. This shared status is one of mutual concern in the different contexts of human relationships [1.9].

This discussion of moral situations recognizes the agent's own conception of "the reality of the situation."[21] An acceptance of this distinction, from the moral point of view, does not imply acceptance of an exclusive dichotomy. For if there were a case in which the agent *constituted* his own situation, the situation so envisaged would also enter into a description of the situation. This possibility of an agent-constituted situation is especially prominent in human affairs as distinct from mere natural events. What we experience in life is often not what happens to us independent of our judgment and choice but what we contribute to it by way of thought and action. There is a basic sense of responsibility involved in being a moral agent. What we enjoy and suffer are often the outcome of what we think and do. These activities are part of the reality of the human situation that can be objectively described from an observer's point of view. What an agent thinks and does figure as ingredients in this description. The agent, though he may fumble, contributes to the reality of the human situation.

3.7 Moral reflection as an activity of apperception may be properly viewed as a step that precedes action. Along with will, intention *(yi)*, and other intellectual acts, the process may be depicted as a *sequence* of steps that eventuates in action or moral performance. On the other hand, if we regard the action retrospectively and view it as an achievement qua achievement, then the steps may appear as *ingredients* rather than mere steps in the process. This reasoning suggests that Wang's disagreement with Chu Hsi on the investigation of things *(ko-wu)* is, in part, a specious one, given our distinction between prospective and retrospective views of moral action [1.9]. The sequential and the nonsequential conceptions appear to be complementary rather than contradictory conceptions of moral action.

The sequential view regards action as the culmination of a series of steps. The model is practical deliberation as a sequential process. At least in the case of self-conscious action, one would expect the agent's action to be an outcome of a number of acts prior to the execution of his intention. Action is a terminus of a process. The nonsequential view, on the other hand, regards action as an object of a moral experience. When one views an action in this way, the steps depicted in the sequential conception can be seen as ingredients in the achievement itself. The question here is not how an action is performed but how it is to be understood as an accomplished deed. Thus while Wang focuses on the unity of prospective knowledge and action or retrospective knowledge, Chu Hsi regards moral learning as a sequence of steps leading to moral achievement.

The two conceptions of action are not incompatible unless each claims to be an exclusive account of human action. But, in a way, the nonsequential conception can claim to be a more illuminating model, provided it assimilates the insight of the sequential conception. It must be noted, however, that the notion of action is subject to process-product ambiguity. The distinction between the two concepts brings this out. The insight of the nonsequential conception lies in its emphasis on action as a *human* action rather than a mere natural event. We would not bother with the process of moral reflection unless there were paradigmatic cases of success in accomplishing our aims. There may be *ideally* a process describable as a sequence of acts, but admitting this requires a proviso that in the case that can be so described, it cannot be regarded as furnishing data that can be generalized into a uniform procedure for moral reflection. Many different sorts of moral reflection may be involved in actions that are responsive to changing circumstances. The procedure involved in each case may be peculiar to the situation at hand rather than an application of a general procedure. Any process leading to an action is yet underdetermined until it is experienced as a deed.

The nature of the action qua action cannot be predicted in advance of the appreciation of a current situation. But this insight, were it to be construed as an insight into the process of moral learning, may mislead pupils into thinking that one can always dispense with methodical learning. A recognition that procedures do not straightaway determine the nature of what one does need not prevent one from appreciating their utility as aids to moral reflection. Moral doing, as a complex affair, cannot be accounted for exclusively by the sequential or nonsequential view of action. In realizing an ideal theme, say *tao* or *jen*, we are dealing not with methods of action but with the complex interplay between prospective and retrospective knowledge [3.4]. This is not to downgrade the insight of Chu Hsi's sequential view of learning as the culmination of a process that consists of a series of steps, particularly with respect to self-cultivation. If learning is a creative process, it is also a process that can be understood in causal terms, though a causal analysis cannot capture the dialectics of moral knowledge and action.

3.8   Summing up, the relevant form of moral reflection in respect of *li* * is an apperceptive activity in a particular situation envisaged by the agent as an occasion for the actualization of his moral vision or *jen*. The appropriate response to a matter at hand is the result of moral reflection. To be a Confucian agent, in light of *jen*, is to take up the role of creative agent. In this conception, creative moral endeavor is akin to an artist's grappling with his initial conception—that is, the problem of making concrete an inchoate idea by way of action mediated through moral reflection. Such a reflection may profit from moral learning and may be regarded as a culmination of such a process, particularly with respect to self-cultivation. In this manner the initial knowledge of what one wants to *do*, the cognitive content of prospective moral knowledge, depends on action for clarification. Thus in addition to *yi*, the volitional and intentional aspect, the transition from prospective to retrospective knowledge also involves a mediation of moral reflection guided by *li**. In this light, intellectual activities such as inquiry and discrimination are constitutive elements of this form of moral reflection [2.1].

3.9   Throughout this chapter, we have been concerned with the coherence of the Confucian vision of *tao* or *jen* and what it means for a person committed to this vision. My explication of Wang's doctrine of the unity of knowledge and action has been deployed to clarify the interaction between prospective and retrospective knowledge. Special attention has been given to the required form of moral reflection in light of *li** as an organic unity making intelligible and plausible the thesis that the exercise of moral agency involves an intellectual aspect in addition to *yi*, the volitional and intentional aspect.[22]

Before we turn to an appraisal of Wang's Confucian vision, it is worthwhile to reformulate more concisely, in a contemporary idiom, his doctrine of the unity of moral knowledge and action. Guided by the distinction between prospective and retrospective moral knowledge, we may regard Wang's doctrine as pointing to certain features of prospective moral knowledge. We may discuss these features in terms of presupposition, precondition, and originating source.

Wang's doctrine can be construed as a conceptual claim for the noncontingent connection between moral knowledge and action. Wang's view that the original substance *(pen-ti)* of knowledge and action is a unity [1.5] can now be rendered as "knowledge and action are intrinsically connected"—that is, knowledge and action are mutually dependent notions. This suggestion is intelligible only when knowledge is viewed prospectively. Prospective knowledge can be said to be a direction of action, and action is the successful effort of prospective knowledge. Given that moral knowledge is practical knowledge, its character cannot be properly understood until the agent appreciates the *point* of having that knowledge in the first place. And to be truly appreciative of this significance is to act in accordance with the relevant content of prospective knowledge. In this way, prospective knowledge is a *presupposition* of action, though the action itself can be an object of retrospective knowledge.

In terms of the cognitive content embedded in aretaic notions, prospective moral knowledge can also be viewed as a *precondition* of action, as expressed in Wang's claim that knowledge is a direction and a beginning of action and action is the successful effort or completion of knowledge [1.10]. For the cognitive content of prospective knowledge is a byproduct of moral learning. And this learning is a precondition for finding the actuating import of moral knowledge. In this way, at issue is the *process* of realizing one's moral learning. The learning serves as both a direction and a beginning of the process of moral endeavor. Of course when the process eventuates in moral achievement, the action can be an object of retrospective knowledge. In terms of intention *(yi)*, prospective knowledge can also be regarded as an *originating source* of action [2.4]. For prospective knowledge is intentional knowledge [3.4], and when the intention is carried out in action it can become an object of retrospective knowledge. Although there are no fixed procedures for effecting the transition from prospective to retrospective knowledge, the elements of will and intention *(yi)*, and the moral reflection attentive to the *li** of particular situations [3.5–3.6], are properly viewed as *constitutive* features of retrospective knowledge.

In this light, Wang's doctrine can be concisely reformulated as a doctrine of the unity of prospective and retrospective moral knowledge. Here we have an ideal rather than a factual description of moral performance. In this sense, Wang's doctrine is "primarily a moral ideal rather than a principle of epistemology."[23] Nevertheless, it is a doctrine of moral psychology that depicts the psychological elements involved in understanding moral achievement or retrospective moral knowledge.

4 *Moral Education, the Language of Vision, and the Problem of Evaluation*

4.1   Before we turn to the problem of evaluating Wang's Confucian vision, let us attend to the pedagogical aspect of Wang's doctrine of the unity of moral knowledge and action. We are told that his "idea arose as an urgent remedial measure."[1] Once he laments over the sick world of his times: "The world today has been morally degenerate. It does not differ from a sick man approaching death."[2] Whether or not the diagnosis is correct, he undoubtedly arrived at his attitude through reflection on his own experience and moral struggle. As Professor Chan instructively points out, "The philosophy of Wang Yang-ming is a vigorous philosophy born of a serious searching and bitter experience."[3] It has been persuasively shown that Wang's doctrine is a culmination of "a series of inner experiences"[4] during the formative period of his life—in Wang's own words, "a hundred deaths and a thousand hardships"—symbolic of "a triumph of Yang-ming's repeated attempts to understand himself."[5] Thus, from the biographical point of view, it is understandable that Wang often insists on personal realization as a key to moral understanding.[6]

While Wang's own experience does contribute to our understanding of his doctrine, it is important to examine his claim that his doctrine is a remedy for a "disease" that infects his world. Regarding the nature of the disease, Wang is quite explicit:

Passage P:
People today distinguish between knowledge and action and pursue them separately, believing that one must know before he can act. They will discuss and learn the business of knowledge first, they say, and wait till they truly know before they put their knowledge into practice. Consequently, to the last day of life, they will never act and also will never know. This doctrine of knowledge first and action later is not a minor *disease* and it did not come about only yesterday. My present advocacy of the unity of knowledge and action is precisely the *medicine* for that disease. The doctrine is not my baseless imagination, for it is the original substance *(pen-ti)* of knowledge and action that they are one. Now that we know this it will do no harm to talk about them separately, for they are only one. If the basic purpose is not understood, however, even if we say they are one, what is the use? It is just idle talk.[7]

Assuming that my explication of Wang's doctrine is plausible, let us inquire in what sense the dichotomy of moral knowledge and action is a disease. Quite clearly, Wang is suggesting that the separate pursuit of moral knowledge and action gives rise to abulia—that is, incapacitation of the agent to will effectively or to make decisions leading to action. Moreover, the dichotomy leads to the view that so long as knowledge and action are exclusive affairs, when I confront a problematic situation of some urgency [2.15], I must first be *assured* intellectually that such and such an act of a certain description is required, say, by an aretaic notion, before I can do anything. And this involves an examination of the cognitive content of moral knowledge before embarking upon a course of action. But if a situation requires immediate attention, to refrain from decision and action is to fail to appreciate the nature of the situation—that is, to fail to engage in moral reflection [3.5]. This failure is markedly a failure in the exercise of moral agency. It is analogous to the case of a physician who hesitates to prescribe medicine because he is unsure of the patient's illness and believes that he must conduct medical research before treating the patient. Wang's analogy is illuminating precisely because moral knowledge and medical knowledge are both species of practical knowledge. For practitioners of morality and medicine to ignore this fact is to convert such forms of knowledge into academic or theoretical knowledge. And in both cases, there is failure to understand the actuating import of practical knowledge. We have here both cases of moral and medical failure in the exercise of agency.

From the pedagogical point of view, the teaching that knowledge comes before doing is liable to give rise to consequences harmful to moral practice. Those who preach such a doctrine not only mislead the learner as to the character of moral knowledge, which is a form of practical knowledge, but also insinuate that unless one is certain one has mastered the subject matter of morality, one should not act. This means that one must be thoroughly familiar with the cognitive content of moral knowledge apart from its actuating import. The insinuation is to be rejected because having moral knowledge is not a matter of possessing either a technical or theoretical competence. It is difficult to make sense of the notion of moral expertise. A competent and responsible exercise of moral agency does not require technical or theoretical expertise. Further, it is arguable that moral problems are not technical problems [2.15]. As Phillips and Mounce point out:

> The "solution" to a moral problem does not stand to moral principles as a solution to a technical problem stands to the principles of technical skill. The "solution" of a moral problem, unlike the solution of a technical problem, cannot be deduced from the principles themselves.[8]

4.2   Wang thus intends his doctrine of the unity of moral knowledge and action as an antidote to moral abulia, but more generally as an emphasis on the necessity of correcting one's moral faults. As an emphasis, however, though plausible from the standpoint of reasonable discourse, it embodies no fixed formulas for correction. The doctrine may be said to emphasize endeavoring to attain and preserving a condition of "moral health" that is responsive to the changing demands of human life. In a revealing letter commenting on a friend's desire to retire from worldly affairs in order to seek *tao*-realization, Wang writes that

> when a good physician treats an illness, he must follow the reality and gravity of the disease, the inside and outside temperatures, before he can decide on medical prescriptions and quantity of drugs. The essential goal being to remove the disease, he does not begin with fixed formulas. This is not different from the nurture of the mind.[9]

The doctrine is thus also a doctrine of moral education. This appears evident in his attitude, as a moral teacher, toward his pupils. Once a pupil said, "I often have regrets." Wang, deploying the medical metaphor, reminded him that "to have regrets and to realize one's mistakes is comparable to medicine. It gets rid of the disease. But it is better to correct one's mistake. If the mistake is allowed to remain, you have a condition in which disease arises because of the medicine."[10] We have reason to believe that his own teaching activity was conducted in a generous spirit—in particular, it was attentive to the use of language in reporting good deeds and moral faults. In one of his reconstructive measures issued after the pacification of the Southern Kiangsi area in 1518,[11] Wang proclaims:

Passage Q:
To display good deeds, the language used must be *clear and decisive*, but in reporting mistakes the language must be *obscure and*

gentle. This is after all the way of liberality and loyalty. If someone has been disrespectful toward his elder brother, do not say so directly, but say that you have heard that he has not done his best in observing the etiquette of serving the elder brother and respecting the elders, that you dare not believe in the report, but that you will tentatively record it and see. This should be the example for all cases of reporting mistakes.[12]

Even when one is affronted by a friend's rude behavior, one should not bear resentment, for such an emotion is incompatible with that of a morally superior person "who helps others to do good."[13] Wang's doctrine may in this way be regarded as aiming at an *inculcation* of concern for others regardless of their misconduct, not an instruction in a fundamental precept for resolving moral problems. This view is quite consistent with his own commitment to *tao* or *jen*. And it is, I believe, rewarding to reflect on the significance of his use of the medical metaphor in the context of commitment to *tao* or *jen* as an ideal theme.

4.3   Let us suppose, without worrying whether or not it is the case, that the knowledge in Wang's doctrine is in some sense the knowledge of an ideal theme—that is, one is cognizant of the actuating import of one's commitment to an ideal theme. As we have observed, a commitment to *jen* as an ideal theme is a commitment to the task of clarifying its significance for the life of the Confucian agent [3.4]. We have here a case of "knowledge by acquaintance" rather than "knowledge by description" in Russell's sense [1.6]. As in the case of knowing a person, much of this knowledge, apart from being inarticulate, is *via negativa*. The agent knows, through his learning, that *tao* or *jen* excludes deliberate cruelty, but he does not know, *via affirmativa*, what constitutes the positive content of *jen*. If he tries to articulate this content in preceptive terms, he is likely to experience utter frustration.[14] And, for Wang, this outcome is expected since *jen* cannot be captured in a set of formulas [2.13]. The search for descriptive knowledge of *jen* is essentially a misguided one, for it is a search after recipes for treating moral ills. One who has a negative knowledge of *jen* is like a Christian who knows the negative injunctions against lying and stealing but has no positive knowledge of what he *ought* to do to promote the ideal of *agape*. Mere knowledge of negative precepts does not aid the agent in arriving at positive action. No positive action, in this way, can be deduced from knowledge *via negativa*.

Thus the agent must in some sense *constitute* the positive content of his ideal theme. When he engages in moral reflection or "reflection on things at hand" [3.5], he is, in effect, specifying in concrete terms, to the best of his current conception, the import of his ideal commitment.[15] In an important sense, *tao* or *jen* as an ideal theme is *vague*, not just because the commitive agent cannot specify it in advance of actual effort to realize it, but because the vagueness is itself a challenge for the agent to constitute its positive content, *via affirmativa*, in the setting of occurrent situations [3.6]—that is, to envisage its requirement as a response to a concrete matter at hand. Put differently, the positive content of the ideal theme is a matter of self-realization or retrospective knowledge of moral achievement. In this way, the agent can learn from his experience of moral faults or failure.

Compare this with medical practice. The physician may be said to have a vague idea of his patients' health. Though he has learned from his medical education the standard diseases (just as the Confucian agent has learned the conventional interpretation of the ideal theme), whether or not this learning has any relevance to his current patient depends on his judgment and experience. But medical knowledge cannot determine, except perhaps in normal cases, what his current patient needs. The physician has to learn from his own medical experiences or past achievement. And this retrospective knowledge of health can improve his medical practice. As he acquires more experience, particularly in unfamiliar cases, he increases his competence at diagnosis and treatment. *Perceptiveness*, informed by past experience, is the key to success as it is in the case of realizing one's commitment to an ideal theme. But no experience of success can pretend to be final, even if the person has for the most part succeeded in the exercise of agency.

This discussion presupposes our distinction between prospective and retrospective knowledge [1.9]. But an exclusive emphasis on retrospective knowledge may be misleading in suggesting that it can be made explicit in a verbal way [3.4]. So also with the notion of negative knowledge of an ideal theme. For Wang, as for any other moral thinker, positive guidance is always provided by paradigmatic individuals and established tradition embedded in Confucian aretaic notions. The point has rather to do with the actuating import of these guiding lights. The actuating import of moral knowledge is thus a continuing affair of reflection and doing. In this way, the separation of the pursuit of moral knowledge from action is more than a minor disease. At issue is not the intelligibility of the distinction between moral knowledge and action but an illegitimate and morally harmful transformation of an ordinary and seemingly innocuous distinction into a dichotomy, thereby creating an unbridgeable gulf between moral knowing and doing.[16] The dichotomy misdirects the efforts of the moral agent to actualize his commitment by suggesting that a morally satisfying and meaningful life is by and large an application of the cognitive content of moral knowledge. Consequently, the dichotomy impels the agent to determine the nature and application of moral knowledge in advance of action that copes with the changing affairs of his life. For a Confucian like Wang, this is what his vision abhors. This naturally raises the question of assessing the Confucian vision. But before we deal with this difficult question, let us note that Wang's insight especially pertains to understanding the nature of moral commitment. It may be objected that such an appreciation of Wang's insight is far from plausible. For the notion of moral commitment suggests a conscious decision concerning the object or ideal of commitment. I admit that the language here is far from felicitous, for commitment in my sense need not be a product of conscious decision. It may simply be an outcome of an awakening experience, like Wang's own, which emerged from the tormenting task of trying to investigate the nature of the bamboo in his earnest hope of realizing sagehood.[17] But the commitment need not be an outcome of personal suffering in the search after meaning in one's life. Sometimes it is more the outcome of a spontaneous awareness in ordinary life—as in the case of the hero in Stefan Zweig's "Transfiguration," who ironically commits a petty theft in concealing another person's winning ticket at a race course and thereafter acquires a vision of common humanity.[18] Or it may be an outcome of free and easy wandering or an experience of awe in nature, as possibly in the cases of Lao Tzu and Chuang Tzu. We can hardly tabulate the variety of sources of nonconscious and nondeliberative moral commitments. Regardless of the source, Wang's contribution does throw light on an important kind of moral commitment, especially when the commitment pertains to an ideal theme like *jen* or a perspective for viewing one's life as a whole.

4.4   In light of the Confucian commitment to *jen* as an ideal theme, Wang's doctrine of the unity of moral knowledge and action provides a concrete exhibition of the possibility of *jen*-realization. It is, so to speak, a scheme for mediation—much more personal and persuasive than the classical Confucian doctrine of rectifying terms—between the Confucian ideal and the actual world.[19] The doctrine brings forth more clearly the basic import of this vision of human excellence and challenges the commitive agent to live and constitute its import in his moral reflection and action. The vision is a continuing target of achievement. There are no moral absolutes to dictate specific courses of action. The essence of the moral life lies in the agent's self-directed becoming. In the course of his earnest struggle, the agent, when successful, can achieve a momentary harmony with the natural order of events. His conception of his own situation in the current setting constitutes preeminently his position in the natural order, and what he does in this setting enters into the constitution of the settled outcome.

The outcome is another natural event, but it carries the indelible stamp of individuality. It is now a *willed event (yi)*. It does not necessarily have a role in human history, but it has its determined status in the agent's past as something he himself has brought about and can be held accountable for. The willed event is thus, in light of *jen*, a fusion of human action and the natural happening. Viewed from this perspective, the natural order contains the moral deed as an integral part, though it is not thereby reducible to a purely moral order. In focusing on the unity of moral knowledge and action, the moral order and the natural order remain distinct but intimately related. In infusing the natural order with a moral concern, the natural order may acquire a moral character.

4.5   At this juncture, a non-Confucian may quite justly raise the query: "How can the Confucian moral vision be assessed as an ideal of human excellence?" This is a most difficult question for any Confucian moral thinker. In Wang's case, we do not receive a clear and direct message that will help us to formulate a plausible answer. Before answering the question, we need some way of understanding the Confucian language of vision—that is, the variety of notions such as *li**, *hsin* (mind), and *li* and their relation to aretaic notions such as filiality, loyalty, and humility. I shall propose a hypothesis concerning the Confucian language of vision and then turn to some of Wang's remarks as data for a coherent and plausible explication; assessment of the Confucian vision is treated in the concluding part of this study [4.12–4.19].[20]

4.6   A moral vision of the relation between human beings and the natural world, as in the case of the Confucian doctrine of the harmony of man and nature, is fundamentally an imaginative conception of an ideal state of affairs—a state of moral excellence. The interpretation of the vision as an ideal theme, rather than an ideal norm, focuses upon the diverse ways of developing the significance of the vision in the lives of individual agents. Thus unlike an ideal norm, the ideal theme leaves open the question of the nature and manner of actualization. As a perspective, it implies some notion of ought-to-be. We may suppose that a reflective agent envisaging an ideal theme is responding to a predicament he has experienced or an actual state of affairs he deems undesirable. It is a troublesome situation to be rectified, a perplexity to be dispelled. His vision of moral excellence is a response that furnishes a way of orienting himself toward his present and future doings. This response thus embodies a judgment of *reflective desirability.* For this response to be more than an empty gesture or mere intellectual act, the agent's judgment of reflective desirability must enter into his conception of moral excellence. His appraisal of his current predicament is not unconnected with his interests, desires, and aspirations. The present situation is unwanted. Instead of resigning himself to living in the situation as he finds it, he wants to do something to it—to change it to something else he regards as satisfactory.[21]

Thus the reflective agent's appraisive response is invested with an active will or intention *(yi)* to transform the actual world in a manner that suits his conception of excellence. For a Confucian visionary, the ideal is intended as a perspective for orientation toward the whole of human life rather than its fragments. What is envisaged is thus a comprehensive and perdurable ideal for viewing human life as a whole.

4.7   The Confucian moral vision of the harmony of man and nature, at its inception, may thus be regarded as an appraisive
conception with an implicit judgment of reflective desirability stemming from the vision as a response to a predicament.
If the visionary engages in discourse about his vision, he must
then articulate it in a manner intelligible to his audience. The
language he employs implicitly contains two features which I
term "responsive sensibility" and "cognitive sense." Responsive sensibility pertains to the visionary's appraisive response
to his predicament involving his needs, desires, and aspirations—in general, his conative and affective interests—coupled with a judgment of reflective desirability. Cognitive
sense, on the other hand, pertains to the intelligibility of the
articulation of the vision in discourse. Engaging in discourse,
the speaker is attempting a "characterization" rather than a
description of his moral vision. Characterization, in my use
of the term, is different from description; it deploys no classificatory terms and thus has no explanatory function or
epistemic status. Instead, it involves "amphibious notions,"
a term I shall elaborate after we attend to characterization.
       A "characterization" of a moral vision exemplifies both the
speaker's responsive sensibility and the cognitive sense of his
utterances. More fully, it contains the following features:

1. Subject matter—that is, an ideal conception of the relation
   between human beings and the natural world
2. An implicit evaluation of the actual world as in some manner unsatisfactory, calling for the vision as an appropriate
   response embodying responsive sensibility
3. A cognitive sense to be elaborated by way of amphibious
   notions
4. An intent to guide the audience toward realization of the
   vision in their lives
5. The vision itself, serving as a unifying perspective for

viewing things in general, inclusive of objects, events, and persons[22]
6. An assumption that the vision is reasonable for anyone who experiences a similar predicament

Since features 1 and 2 have already been discussed in our examination of moral vision and are moreover important for the amphibious notions dealt with in the next section [4.8], we shall attend here to the remaining features. Let us focus on features 4, 5, and 6 and leave 1, 2, and 3 as background conditions.

We may say that in characterizing his vision the speaker is engaged in *persuasive* discourse—that is, he is attempting to articulate his moral vision persuasively. To characterize a vision is to provide an audience with a practical understanding of the vision as a guide to actual conduct. I assume here that the Confucian speaker is a commitive thinker and not a moral theorist concerned with developing a systematic doctrine of morality in normative ethics or metaethics [3.2]. Thus his primary purpose for engaging in characterization is to present his vision as a *viable* one for adoption (feature 4). Moreover, the vision itself is a *unifying perspective* for viewing things in general. Feature 5 is suggested by our consideration of *li** in *t'iao-li** [2.17] and *i-li** [1.16]. In this light, characterization does not aim at a description of objects, events, or states of affairs, though in a particular context of discourse some such description is presupposed. In other words, the vision is a unifying perspective for dealing with any putative description.

The underlying assumption in feature 6 is necessary for assuring that this persuasive discourse is not rhetorical in the pejorative sense but a *reasonable* one—a feature that is of utmost importance for evaluating the Confucian vision. We shall turn to this question later [4.12]. This feature captures two main themes in Wang: that *tao* is amenable to public discussion [2.13] and a matter of personal realization.²³ Persuasive discourse is, in this way, reasonable, for it is open to public discussion where an exchange of reasons between speaker and audience is expected. There appears to be no final arbiter for this open-ended sort of discourse.²⁴ But it may be assumed that the participants in a discourse articulating moral vision have a vital mutual interest at stake, since the vision is supposed to be an answer to a perplexing human predicament. Disagreements are bound to occur, but they are more the means for developing a satisfactory articulation of the vision than disputable issues based on contending theses.

4.8 Let us now take up the third feature of characterization: cognitive sense. A moral vision, as we have seen, has a cognitive sense in that it can be rendered intelligible in the context of communication. By way of what I call "amphibious notions," the moral vision, given the responsive sensibility as a background, can be set forth in clear terms. A characterization quite obviously has an *expressive* aspect, for it contextually implies that the speaker is committed to the vision. In an important sense, the cognitive aspect of his vision is an intelligible articulation of a moral commitment. As I conceive them, amphibious notions are not mere tools but *constitutive means* for such an articulation;²⁵ for each use of amphibious notions in itself constitutes the cognitive content of the statement, and, consequently, the use binds the speaker in subsequent discourse involving the same context. Hence amphibious notions are not ad hoc devices invoked for occasional use.

I shall introduce the concept of amphibious notions by way of commenting on Fogelin's treatment of what he calls "amphibious statements." Suppose that an anthropologist says: "The natives are now asking their rain god Lorba to replenish their wells, illustrating once more the tendency to project through deification persistent cultural needs." According to Fogelin:

In the first half of this sentence a description is offered from the perspective of the natives engaged in the ritual; in the second half of the sentence a judgment is made from an entirely different perspective, that of the speaker himself.[26]

Amphibious statements are thus for Fogelin the simultaneous application of two different but compatible perspectives on the same subject. In characterizing moral vision, amphibious notions also display, from the analytical point of view, two different perspectives which may be labeled "descriptive" and "evaluative"; but in addition, since the vision is a unifying perspective, an amphibious notion is a *unitary* expression of the vision. It is, so to speak, not so much a conjunction as an intersection of two compatible perspectives—or, better, an intercalation between two perspectives by one single overall perspective. We can, for example, interpret Wang's saying that *"tao* is *(chi)* Heaven *(t'ien)"* by construing "Heaven" as an amphibious notion that deploys *tao* as a unifying perspective for viewing all living and nonliving things under heaven or in the world. This way of interpreting *tao* makes sense of an otherwise puzzling remark in the same context. After pointing out that *tao* cannot be pinned down in specific terms [2.13], Wang goes on:

Passage R:
Take those people today who talk about Heaven. Do they actually understand it? It is incorrect to say that the sun, the moon, wind, and thunder constitute Heaven. It is also incorrect to say that man, animals, and plants do not constitute it. *Tao* is *(chi)* Heaven.[27]

Whether or not the present interpretation is plausible depends on our examination of the various quasi-identity expressions in Wang's articulation of his Confucian vision. To this topic we shall attend shortly.

Amphibious notions, as the term suggests, straddle, from the conceptual point of view, two apparently distinct domains of discourse. On the one hand, they purport to say something about things in the world—that is, in some sense they offer us a description of things. On the other hand, since they involve the moral vision as a unifying perspective, they also evaluate things in the world. The first function does not refer to factual description but is an empathic reminder that any putative description is subject to a redescription in terms of the unifying perspective. And when the second function enters as a constitutive element of the redescription, we have, in effect, an *ideal redescription* of the items in the original description. But no detailed ideal redescription need be given, since the *tao*, for example, cannot be specified in any determinate set of formulas.

Amphibious notions may also be regarded as "focal notions" for focusing on certain aspects of the world deserving of attention. These notions are much like aesthetic concepts as Saw conceives them. According to Saw, "The point of concepts used in aesthetic discourse is to direct our attention to the important features of the work. These features are important in the sense that if they were not noticed, the work would not be appreciated."[28] Similarly, we can say that amphibious notions used in a discourse on moral vision direct our attention to the important features of the vision. If these features were not noticed, the vision would not be appreciated; when they are noticed, they also constitute our understanding of the moral vision.

In this light, amphibious notions serve as *amplifications* of a moral vision. Alternatively, they may be called "ampliative notions." The moral vision, as it is initially conceived, may be quite vague, and clarification by way of amphibious notions enables both speaker and audience to attain a cognitive understanding of the expanding and enriching nature of the vision. Moreover, since the vision is an ideal perspective on the whole of human life, amphibious notions provide an expansive horizon for the actuating import of the commitment to moral vision.[29] In light of this discussion of characterization and amphibious notions, I can now state concisely my hypothesis concerning the Confucian language of vision as deployed by Wang:

> The Confucian language of moral vision is a characterization involving amphibious notions which serve fundamentally as amplifications of both the cognitive sense and actuating import of the moral vision as a unifying perspective on the whole of human life.

4.9   This hypothesis, it is hoped, will enable us to offer a plausible explication of a series of quasi-identity expressions such as "*tao* is *(chi)* Heaven" and "mind *(hsin)* is *(chi)* *li**." But before we turn to these quasi identities, let us first note that the construal of *tao* as a unifying perspective applies to such an expression as "*tao* is one."[30] Of course, Wang at times also uses such expressions as "mind is one"[31] and "*li** is one,"[32] but these expressions seem to depend on the relation of mind and *li** to *tao*. For *li** as in *tao-li**, we have no problem if we are correct in claiming that *tao* can function as an ideal reason— that is, as a reasonable perspective to adopt [2.13]. It cannot be denied that these expressions suggest, in light of medieval philosophy, that "one" is a transcendental term with a metaphysical or ontological reference.[33] I shall not pursue this sort of reconstruction, which goes beyond the scope of this study. Nevertheless it is possible, with a minimal metaphysical commitment, to admit that it is a transcendental term like "the good," functionally equivalent to the Confucian "highest good" *(chih-shan)* as a regulative ideal for which moral vision is offered in the first place. Instead of being a constitutive feature of the moral life, we may say with Emmet that it is a regulative ideal that "marks out a direction of improvement, not the prospect of an achieved adequacy."[34] *Tao* as a unifying perspective is a perspective for continuing moral improvement.

4.10 In the course of preparing this study, I was deeply perplexed by the problem of rendering intelligible a series of expressions that appear as quasi identities like the expression "*tao* is *(chi)* t'ien.*" My hypothesis is designed to deal with this problem [4.8]. But for this hypothesis to be plausible I have to assume that *tao* admits of alternative linguistic designations. This assumption seems justified in passage M, which I cited in discussing *i-li** [2.16].[35] Given this assumption, let us consider the following quasi identities:

1. "*Tao* is *(chi)* Heaven *(t'ien)*."
2. "Mind *(hsin)* is *(chi)* tao.*"
3. "Mind *(hsin)* is *(chi)* li*.*"
4. "*Li* [ritual propriety] is *(chi)* li*.*"[36]

In each case, the difficulty is posed by the particle *chi,* which seems innocuous enough when rendered in terms of the English verb "to be." Ching justly reminds us that "the Chinese language lacks a definite verb *to be,*" but she goes on to say that "the proposition, *hsin chi li**—literally, *hsin* and *li** are one and the same—can be translated as "the source of all being and virtue lies in *hsin,* in man's mind-and-heart."[37] I have no desire to question the correctness of this metaphysical rendering, but it is a clear case of interpretation of the particle *chi.* And one may wonder how two terms such as *hsin* and *li*,* which are literally "one and the same," get so transposed by the metaphysical reading. I have no doubt that *chi* has the force of "is the same as," but such a proposed functional equivalent for *chi* needs to be clarified. As Austin observes, there are a few distinct cases of "calling different sorts of things by the same name" which cannot be reduced to the notion of similarity or, for that matter, to the notion of identity.[38] I have thus called expressions 1 to 4 "quasi identities" as a warning not to regard them as statements of synonyms (which no scholar of Wang, to my knowledge, has done). But if these are not statements of synonyms, how are they properly rendered in terms of the verb "to be"?

The verb "to be" is ambiguous. It may refer, for example, to identity, to inclusion, or to predication. Since identity in both logical and semantic senses is clearly inapplicable to Wang, one may try inclusion. If this course is taken, one has to ascribe to Wang the view that mind and *li* (ritual propriety) are both included in *li**. This would make *li** a class term, thus suggesting a view completely contrary to our explication of *li** [2.10–2.18]. Moreover, this view implies that *li** is external to the mind—a thesis Wang explicitly rejects [2.17].[39] The remaining alternative is predication. If this is appropriate, we have to construe the terms on the right-hand side of the expressions as adjectives. That would make Heaven, for example, an attribute of *tao*. This is an interesting course to pursue, but I shall not attempt it here. Instead, I regard the terms as substantives and propose that *chi* in all four cases is a particle functioning as a demonstrative—that is, one term can make manifest certain aspects of the reference of another term. Our assumption that "*tao* admits of alternative linguistic designations" can be rephrased in the material mode of speech as "*tao* has alternative or various manifestations." In following this course, I am essentially guided by the distinction between "the latent *(yin)*" and "the manifest *(hsien)*" in the opening section of the *Doctrine of the Mean* [2.12]. *Tao* is the latent or "the hidden" in that its full significance cannot be comprehended; when it is occasionally comprehended in discourse, the understanding is merely partial. In Wang's words, "*Tao* cannot be exhausted with any sense of completion" [2.12]. Nevertheless, it does have manifestations that can be generally understood. Construing *chi* as having a demonstrative function, we can simply recast the four expressions in the preceding paragraph as follows:

1a. "*Tao* is manifested in Heaven."
2a. "Mind manifests *tao*."
3a. "Mind manifests *li**."
4a. "*Li* (ritual propriety) manifests *li**."

For expression 1a we can further explain that *tao* has a significant aspect that is manifested in all things under heaven—that is, as a unifying perspective for dealing with all things in the world. This gives us an understanding of the general action-guiding function of *tao*, but the guidance cannot in this way be further specified in advance of the agent's confrontation with the actual situation. Expression 2a draws attention to *tao*, an ideal theme, as it is manifested in the mind's active concern with things [2.17]. It is an object of our will and intention *(yi)* or active commitment [2.3–2.4]. If the mind thus manifests *tao*, then it must have succeeded in its effort in whatever it is engaged in doing. In terms of Wang's doctrine of moral knowledge and action, expression 2a draws attention to the unity of prospective and retrospective knowledge [2.7]. For expression 3a, we can construe it to mean that *li** is a manifestation of the reasonable aspect of the mind's commitment to *tao* [2.19]. Similarly, expression 4a points to the reasonableness of *li* (ritual propriety) in terms of *tao*.

Following my hypothesis and assumption [4.8], we can say that the notions of heaven, mind, and *li** are amphibious notions that *amplify* the different aspects of *tao* as a unifying perspective. In other words, the Confucian moral vision can be grasped by way of amphibious notions. The manifestations of *tao*, however, are not logically or practically equivalent; whereas the mind focuses on an active concern for the realization of the vision, *li** focuses on the reasonable aspect of the mind's commitment to *tao* and *li* (propriety) focuses on compliance with ritual rules as a reasonable constitutive strategy for the realization of *tao*. But notably these various manifestations can also be taken as lower-level perspectives that can be simultaneously deployed. In expression 3a, for instance, we may say that *tao* interposes and connects two different lower perspectives—that is, will and moral reflection guided by *li** [3.5]. We have here, as it were, an intersection between two perspectives effected by *tao* as a unifying perspective. If this reconstruction is admissible, then *tao* as a unifying perspective has various significant manifestations captured by the aretaic notions via the lesser generic terms or amphibious notions, since the latter are further specifiable in aretaic notions [2.11]. The aretaic notions may also be said to be invested, indirectly, with *tao*; consequently, they are all ideal-embedded notions. As a unifying perspective, *tao* is one thread that joins a variety of greater or lesser manifestations. In Wang's words: "The *tao* of the Sage is the great mean and perfect correctness, penetrating both the higher and the lower levels, being one thread that runs through all."[40]

4.11   Throughout this study, I have used *tao* and *jen* as interchangeable terms for discussing Wang's moral vision, but I have not implied that they are semantically equivalent. *Tao* and *jen*, in general, differ in the direction of semantic stress, to borrow a term from Wheelwright.[41] *Jen* stresses the significance of the moral vision as residing in affectionate human relationships, a habitat which is capable of indefinite expansion and ultimately embraces the whole universe; *tao* stresses the ongoing course of changing circumstances that calls for an exercise of the agent's sense of rightness (*i*) in coping with them. For understanding Wang's Confucian vision, the difference between *tao* and *jen* is not important. What is important is that the penetrating and expansive significance of the vision can be made manifest, through the commitive agent's efforts, in dealing with all things.

We may also observe that as a unifying perspective in cognitive understanding, *tao* or *jen* can also be amplified by way of other apparently amphibious notions—such as equilibrium *(chung)*, for focusing on what *tao* is like when it is occasionally realized in one's life, or *liang-chih*, for focusing on the innate capacity for realizing the vision. The latter, however, is especially problematic to elaborate, for Wang also thinks of *liang-chih* as an intuitive knowledge of the good. It is not clear what version of ethical intuitionism can be plausibly explicated on his behalf without getting into the difficulties that beset this type of doctrine in moral philosophy. One advantage of my hypothesis is that it frees Wang's moral vision from entanglement in the problems of ethical intuitionism.[42] Moreover, the hypothesis makes coherent sense of Wang's vision without an involvement in the metaphysical issues that surround his conception of mind in relation to its apparently external and independently existent objects. More important, the hypothesis paves the way for evaluating the acceptability of Wang's vision, to which we shall devote our attention in concluding this study.

4.12 If a person were to detach himself from concern with the question of evaluation, the Confucian vision of the harmony of man and nature could well be an interesting subject of intellectual entertainment. James writes that "a man's vision is the great fact about him. . . . A philosophy is an expression of a man's intimate character, and all definitions of the universe are but deliberately adopted reactions of human characters upon it."[43] We have ground to believe that Wang would not approve of this attitude toward his works, for as he reminds one of his critics, *tao* is a proper subject for discussion [2.13].[44] Thus the question of evaluation is in order. There is, however, a difficulty in dealing with this question, for evaluation calls for a detailed study of Wang's vision in comparison with other visions. This far-reaching axiological task cannot be attempted here.[45] Instead, in this closing section I shall gather together and amplify certain features of this study in order to prepare the way for an appropriate evaluation by comparative moral philosophers. I center my attention on the question of justifying the adoption of the Confucian vision. Justifying the adoption of a moral vision is a question of *vindication* rather than validation of claims to moral knowledge in respect of given moral norms or principles.[46] Earlier in this chapter [4.7] I set forth the assumption that "the vision is reasonable for anyone who experiences a similar predicament." Involved in this assumption are the notions of experience and reasonableness. Whether or not an agent is vindicated in his adoption of the vision crucially depends on his understanding of these notions.

4.13   Experience plays a dual role in the characterization of Confucian vision: as *antecedent* to the envisaging of the vision and as *consequent* to the conduct lived in light of the vision. The experience of a perplexing predicament, and more especially of the gap between man and his world, furnishes an occasion for the conception. Since the Confucian vision is largely guided by the notion of harmony in its articulation, we can suppose that the thinker himself has also experienced instances of harmony within his life. If the experience of the gap is an occasion for the inception of the vision, the experience of harmony, however confined in its character, must furnish a source for the conception. In this way, the antecedent experience embraces both the occasion and its source. The source itself must be deemed by the thinker as eminently desirable on reflection. The vision itself may be regarded as an *ideal projection* of particular experiences or elementary experiences of the harmony of man and his world.

In *consequent* experience of the vision, the thinker finds a vindication in his own adoption of the vision. Thus for Wang the ultimate vindication lies in consequent rather than in antecedent experience. In an important sense, it is living out the actuating import of the vision that bears witness to the truth of Wang's vision. Wang would have thus endorsed the view that "that which provides the 'verification' of a world view is not an object of experience, but the nature of the experience itself, the relation which it involves between the self and its world."[47] We must add, however, that such an experience is an object of retrospective knowledge; and when it is articulated, it is subject to public discussion and assessment.

If an auditor shares the antecedent experience with the speaker, he has a basis for adopting the vision. But whether this is a sufficient reason for adopting it depends on a judgment of reflective desirability made by his responsive sensibility [4.7]. Although this is a question only the concerned agent can answer for himself, a few factors are clearly involved. In the first place, the viability of the vision depends on the agent's character and ability to realize the vision within his life. In effect, the agent needs to ask: "Given my present character and circumstance, can I carry out the task involved in the vision?" If the answer is negative, is he willing to transform his present character and circumstance in light of the vision [2.3]? Even if the agent shares with the speaker the antecedent experience of harmony, the experience itself may not be viewed as an answer to his predicament, for he may have none; the experience may be nothing more than a gratuitous satisfaction that has no import for his life as a whole.

Perhaps most important, the agent must ask himself whether he can wholeheartedly *identify* himself with the vision when it is adopted. Can he reflectively desire the vision as constitutive of his second-order volition in such a way that the vision is an answer to his perplexity over human life as a whole [2.6]? The answers to these questions presuppose that the agent has a capacity to evaluate his own dispositions, desires, and circumstances. Together these factors point to the conative aspect of vindication. And to this aspect we may also add the affective factor—the agent's capacity to delight in the experience of harmony or find joy and security in light of the vision.[48]

4.14 The cognitive aspect of vindication lies in *reasonableness* as contrasted with the standard notion of *rationality*, that is, compliance with the canons of inductive and deductive reasoning. Although the two notions are sometimes used interchangeably, Perelman points out:

> We understand the expression rational deduction as conformity to the rules of logic, but we cannot speak of a reasonable deduction. On the contrary, we can speak of a reasonable compromise and not of a rational compromise. At times the two terms are applicable but in a different sense: a rational decision can be unreasonable and vice versa.[49]

If the distinction between rationality and reasonability appears intuitively clear, the latter is still difficult to discuss in a systematic way. For obviously, as a distinct notion, it cannot be explicated in terms of norms or precepts. It is, moreover, questionable whether any normative attempt at a definition can be intelligible. For if such a definition is given, there is no need for attending to it as a distinctive notion. We can simply retain the term as a synonym for rationality or else as a special form of rationality that involves factors in addition to inductive and deductive canons. And in Wang's case, especially, such an attempt is completely contrary to his notions of *tao-li** and *i-li** [2.13–2.16].

In the concluding part of our study of the notion of *li**, I suggested that in a compendious way *li** can be rendered as "reasonableness" [2.19]. The problem now is to articulate clearly what is involved in the Confucian conception of reasonableness. In this task we are guided by Aristotle's procedure in explaining his notion of practical wisdom. Says Aristotle, "We may approach the subject of practical wisdom by studying the persons to whom we attribute it."[50] Similarly, we shall inquire into the subject of reasonableness by studying the persons who are said to possess this quality. But it must be observed that such a study is notably an ideal reconstruction rather than a factual description of the quality of reasonableness, though it involves rather obvious considerations drawn from common experiences of moral agents. In this brief inquiry, I center on considerations derived from my reflections on certain features of Wang's ethics and Confucian ethics in general. The discussion to be offered does not pretend to be a novel contribution or an exhaustive treatment of this topic; it is, rather, a reminder that assessment of the Confucian vision depends on giving due weight to the notion of reasonableness.[51]

4.15 One characteristic of a reasonable person is open-mindedness or impartiality. This is an attitude which Confucius regards as a quality of the superior man. He says of himself, "I have no course for which I am predetermined, and no course against which I am predetermined."[52] On this attitude of impartiality Wang is quite explicit, apart from his stress that *tao* is amenable to public discussion [4.1]. On one occasion when Hsün Tzu is criticized for maintaining that "to nourish the mind there is nothing better than sincerity," Wang makes the following observation:

Passage S:
Though there are many defects in what Hsün Tzu said, one should not seize upon one incident in order to find fault with him. Generally speaking, if in examining the sayings of anyone one has a preconceived opinion, he will be wrong. Though the saying, "He who seeks to be rich will not be humane," was uttered by the wicked official Yang Hu, Mencius quoted it just the same. This shows how impartial sages and worthies are.[53]

In discussion one must be impartial as a judge hearing a case
—attentive to weak and strong points in the dispute so that a
just decision can be rendered in the case at hand.[54] This analogy suggests strongly that impartiality involves a respect for
evidence and a willingness to revise one's opinion when it is
confronted by contrary evidence.[55] This attitude, however,
has nothing to do with the question of whether one must uni-
versalize one's moral beliefs for them to have a characteristic
reasonableness. It is more closely related to the Confucian notion of extensive concern for others.

4.16   For Confucius, as for Wang, extensive concern for others
rooted in filiality and fraternal piety is the method of realizing *jen*.[56] "A man of *jen*, desiring to establish his own character, also establishes the character of others, and desiring to
be prominent himself, also helps others to be prominent."[57]
Whether or not one accepts this method for realizing moral
vision, the quality is what we ordinarily expect of a reasonable person. In respect of characterization as a form of Confucian discourse, the focus here is on loyalty to one's own
commitment and the concern for others implied in the varying remarks in the *Analects* on *chung** and *shu*. *Chung** pertains to the seriousness and sincerity of one's moral commitment; *shu* pertains especially to concern for conduct as it
affects other persons.

These notions of *chung** and *shu* imply an acknowledgment of a respect for reciprocity, commonly expressed in the
Golden Rule. But unlike the Christian, the Confucian stress
on self-regarding and other-regarding conduct is an extension
of personal regard to other persons. Moreover, the concern
for others is part of the concern for oneself as a reasonable
agent. This means that the needs, desires, and aspirations of
others—that is, their responsive sensibility—are an important
part of a person's preoccupation with his own moral condition. This is what makes sense of extending one's own con-

cern. When one's own interests conflict with others', the reasonable person views the conflict as capable of reconciliation —not just in the sense of compromise, but in the sense that people are to be joined in friendship. Thus extensive concern for others is not simply a matter of showing respect for their responsive sensibility; more important, it is a matter of attempting to embrace others within the ambience of one's personal relationships. The desire involved is a second-order desire [2.6], which implies that one should act toward others as he would expect others to behave toward him.[58] The important point to observe is that a reasonable agent is one who has some standard of behavior whether or not he applies it to all other persons. *Chung**, as loyalty to one's own commitment, is a commitment to a standard for guiding conduct. And given the second-order desire for extensive concern for others, it is also a desire to follow one's own standard. And when this desire is coupled with the characteristic of impartiality, the standard is open to revision in confrontation with others.

4.17 A reasonable person is one whose judgment and conduct are imbued with a sense of *appropriateness*. Our discussion of *i-li**, it is hoped, brings out quite clearly the sense of appropriateness with respect to an occurrent situation [2.16]. This characteristic is not unconnected with impartiality, for the latter is a preparation for the Confucian stress on the necessity of moral reflection or reflection on things at hand—a notion in fact suggested in a remark of Tzu-hsia in the *Analects*.[59] As we have seen, moral reflection is preeminently an activity of apperceiving the situation as a whole [3.5]. This sense of appropriateness *(i)* does not preclude a concern with consequences of one's conduct in light of one's commitment, but one may experience a change of heart on account of one's sense of appropriateness in coping with changing circumstances.

Nor is one's sense of appropriateness completely detached

from the context of conventional moral practice; for a moral act is a social act, and to the extent that one complies with social conventions in accord with one's sense of appropriateness, the act is properly deemed a conventional act. Insofar as a reasonable agent is expected to conform to conventions, given his characteristic impartiality, his attitude toward the conventions at issue is a cautious and sometimes a critical one. As Wang writes: "While a gentleman does not follow customs or conventions lightly, neither does his mind differ from custom."[60] On another occasion, Wang counsels the correspondent not to compromise his moral integrity by complying with conventional practice.[61] It must be noted that for the Confucian, where the conventions pertain to ritual rules *(li)*, it is important to pay heed to them if only as a way of expressing one's humility, or more generally a sense of decency or civility. But again, whether or not one must comply with ritual rules in a particular situation is a question for *i* or the sense of appropriateness. The ritual requirements must be judged relevant before one assents to them in particular cases. Sense of appropriateness is the preeminent characteristic of a reasonable person. If it is absent, a person can hardly be called reasonable even if he possesses the other characteristics.

4.18   A reasonable person is also imbued with a sense of *moderation*. This is clearly implied in the notion *chung* (equilibrium), which can also be rendered as the mean (as in the *Doctrine of the Mean*). It is a mean between excess and deficiency.[62] To Confucius was attributed this saying:

> Shun was indeed a man of great wisdom! He loved to question others and to examine their words, however ordinary. He concealed what was bad in them and displayed what was good. He took hold of their two extremes, took the mean between them, and applied it in dealing with the people. This was how he became Shun [the sage-emperor].[63]

The mean here especially pertains to feelings such as pleasure, anger, sorrow, and joy as in the state of congeniality, so to speak; and when feelings are expressed in particular settings, they must be harmonious. This is the conception set forth in the opening section of the *Doctrine of the Mean*. For Wang, equilibrium and harmony are not contrastive and opposed psychological states. As he points out:

> *Passage T:*
> It should not be said that all ordinary persons have attained the state of equilibrium before the feelings are aroused. For "substance and function come from one source." Given the substance, there is function, and given the equilibrium before the feelings are aroused, there is harmony in which the feelings are aroused and all attain due measure and degree.[64]

Although the doctrine of equilibrium and harmony is a partial articulation of Wang's vision, the stress on moderation with respect to one's passions and desires is recognized as an essential condition for realization of the vision. This aspect of Confucian ethics has a striking affinity with Aristotle's famous discussion of moral virtues as means. It is even more interesting to note that coupled with the sense of appropriateness, the mean for Wang, as for Aristotle, is not something determined in advance of engagement with particular situations [2.16].[65]

4.19 In addition to impartiality, concern for others, and a sense of appropriateness and moderation, a reasonable person appreciates the actuating import of the cognitive content of practical knowledge. The nature of this appreciation is the question that underlies Wang's doctrine of the unity of moral knowledge and action—the question that occasioned this study [1.1]. If we now ask what is involved in vindicating one's adoption of the Confucian vision or characterizing the Confucian vision, we can point out that aside from the conative and affective factors, the agent or the audience must also be reasonable—that is, possess the characteristics of impartiality, extensive concern for others, sense of appropriateness and moderation, and appreciation of the actuating import of the cognitive content of practical knowledge. Of course, the Confucian may well adopt his vision without actually possessing all these qualities. Given intelligence and fortunate circumstance, one can become a reasonable moral agent so long as one has a firm determination to attain the highest good [2.3]. To assess the Confucian vision, however, one must reflect on this notion of reasonable vindication. What more is involved apart from the characteristics of reasonableness? This remains an important question for moral theory.

This study of Wang's doctrine of the unity of moral knowledge and action succeeds, I hope, in showing Wang's contributions to moral psychology. These contributions, though in need of more detailed inquiry into the psychological aspects of moral agency, are at least illustrative of the elementary considerations that demand attention from philosophers concerned with formulating an adequate moral psychology.

Notes

Introduction

1. J. L. Austin, "A Plea for Excuses," *Philosophical Papers*, 2nd ed. (Oxford: Clarendon Press, 1961), p. 178. Incidentally, a Confucian should find congenial Austin's remark that "ethics are *not*, as philosophers are prone to assume, simply in the last resort *physical movements*: very many of them have the general character, in whole or in part, of conventional or ritual acts, and are therefore, among other things, exposed to infelicity." See *How to Do Things with Words* (Cambridge: Harvard University Press, 1962), pp. 19–20. (For my own studies on *li*, see "Dimensions of *Li* (Propriety): Reflections on an Aspect of Hsün Tzu's Ethics," *Philosophy East and West*, vol. 29, no. 4 (1979); and "*Li* and Moral Justification: A Study in the *Li Chi*," *Philosophy East and West*, forthcoming.

2. Ibid., pp. 193–194, 200–201.

3. Thus in 1958 Anscombe maintained that "it is not profitable for us at present to do moral philosophy . . . until we have an adequate philosophical psychology." Such notions as "action," "intention," "pleasure," and "wanting," for example, should be examined before we take up the notion of virtue. See G.E.M. Anscombe, "Modern Moral Philosophy," *Philosophy* (1958), reprinted in G. Wallace and A.D.M. Walker (eds.), *The Definition of Morality* (London: Methuen, 1970), pp. 211 and 228. The importance of exploring the connection between moral philosophy and the philosophy of mind is also explicit in Stuart Hampshire, *Thought and Action* (London: Chatto and Windus, 1959).

4. For example: A. E. Murphy, *The Theory of Practical Reason* (LaSalle: Open Court, 1965); D. Z. Phillips and H. O. Mounce, *Moral Practices* (London: Routledge & Kegan Paul, 1969); Peter Winch, *Ethics and Action* (London: Routledge & Kegan Paul, 1972); Bernard Williams, *Problems of*

the Self (Cambridge: Cambridge University Press, 1973); Alan Donagan, *The Theory of Morality* (Chicago: University of Chicago Press, 1977); A. I. Melden, *Rights and Persons* (Berkeley and Los Angeles: University of California Press, 1978); Richard Brandt, *A Theory of the Good and the Right* (New York: Oxford University Press, 1979); and Peter French, *The Scope of Morality* (Minneapolis: University of Minnesota Press, 1979).

5. "Moral psychology" refers to the exploration of the relation from a moral philosopher's point of view. The connection, of course, can also be explored from the point of view of the philosophy of mind. In this case, we may be concerned with such questions as whether the concept of person or agency is a normative notion and, if so, how it is related to the notion of moral person or moral agency as it is deployed in moral philosophy. Can the concept of an action be explicated without a consideration of responsibility—more particularly, moral responsibility?

6. Throughout this study I construe *chih* as moral knowledge, leaving open the question of how this moral knowledge is related to factual knowledge, a topic that borders on moral epistemology rather than moral psychology. For a challenging discussion of this problem, particularly in connection with the notion of innate knowledge of the good, see T'ang Chün-i, *Chung-kuo che-hsüeh yüan-lun, tao-lun p'ien*, 3rd ed. (Taipei: Hsüeh-sheng shu-chü, 1978), chap. 10, pp. 340–347.

7. Throughout this essay references are to Wing-tsit Chan's translation and sectional arrangement of *Ch'uan-hsi lu* entitled *Instructions for Practical Living and Other Neo-Confucian Writings by Wang Yang-ming* (New York: Columbia University Press, 1963), hereafter cited as *Instructions*. I have also made use of Julia Ching's *The Philosophical Letters of Wang Yang-ming* (Columbia: University of South Carolina Press, 1972), hereafter cited as *Letters*. The Chinese text I have consulted is *Wang Yang-ming ch'uan-shu* (Taipei: Cheng-chung Book Co., 1955). Occasionally I have also made use of Frederick Goodrich Henke (trans.), *The Philosophy of Wang Yang-ming* (New York: Paragon Book Reprint Corp., 1964). With the exception of moral knowledge *(chih)* and action *(hsing)*, I have throughout retained the transcriptions of key terms such as *yi, hsin, li**, and others that require explication in the context of the doctrine of the unity of moral knowledge and action. Minor emendations of existing translations are indicated by asterisks following page references or explained by notes. Asterisks are also used in transcriptions to distinguish homophones of different Chinese characters.

8. While Wang's doctrine of mind quite plausibly offers a case for metaphysical reconstruction, his doctrine of *liang-chih*, for a moral philosopher, appears to be puzzling. Though it can be construed as a form of ethi-

cal intuitionism, it is unclear to me how this doctrine can be intelligibly and plausibly restated in relation to the standard versions of ethical intuitionism in Western philosophy. Certain remarks of Wong point to perceptual intuitionism akin to an aspect of Richard Price's moral philosophy; but others seem to point to affinity with philosophical intuitionism like that of Sidgwick. I believe that a coherent reformulation of the notion of *liang-chih* depends on an understanding of the doctrine of *chih-hsing ho-i* and also more basically on the doctrine of mind. It is perhaps best to avoid the label "intuitionism" and simply attend to the role of *liang-chih* in relation to Wang's comprehensive philosophy of mind, which, as Cheng has shown, is rooted in his metaphysics of mind. And when we construe the mind as essentially moral in character, we can also plausibly maintain with Mou that Wang's total philosophy is a "moral metaphysics" as distinct from Kant's metaphysics of morals. See Chung-ying Cheng, "Unity and Creativity in Wang Yang-ming's Philosophy of Mind," *Philosophy East and West*, vol. 23, nos. 2–3 (1973); and Mou Tsung-san, *Hsin-ti yü hsing-ti*, vol. 1 (Taipei: Cheng-chung shu-chü, 1973), chap. 3. For a straightforward exposition of Wang's "moral metaphysics," see Liu Chen-hsiu, "Yang-ming hsin-hsüeh shu-p'ing," in *Annals of Philosophy*, no. 2 (1962).

9. Carsun Chang, *Wang Yang-ming: Idealist Philosopher of Sixteenth-Century China* (Jamaica: St. John's University Press, 1962), p. 39.

10. This question seems to depend on one's approach to Wang's philosophy as a whole. Liang, for instance, places utmost importance on the doctrine by regarding the four characters *chih-hsing ho-i* as representing the whole of Wang's philosophy. According to him the rest of Wang's works are but footnotes to these four characters. See Liang Chi-chao, *Wang Yang-ming chih-hsing ho-i chi chao* (Taipei: Chung-hua shu-chü, 1968), p. 5. Another view, taking mind *(hsin)* as a basic concept, construes the doctrine as a conclusion of Wang's theory of mind. See Lo Kuang "Wang Yang-ming lun-hsin," *Yang-ming hsüeh lun-wen chih* (Taipei: Huakang, 1976), p. 41. Along similar lines but better supported by elaborate arguments, Cheng regards the doctrine as "a demonstration of the unity and creativity of mind" (Cheng, "Unity and Creativity," p. 58). Focusing on Wang's quest for sagehood, the doctrine, it is suggested, may be regarded as a symbolization of Wang's "repeated attempts to understand himself." See Wei-ming Tu, *Neo-Confucian Thought in Action: Wang Yang-ming's Youth (1472–1509)* (Berkeley and Los Angeles: University of California Press, 1976), p. 175. Similar emphasis is found in Julia Ching, *To Acquire Wisdom* (New York: Columbia University Press, 1976). With the exception of Liang and Tu, most of these writers find it essential to connect the doctrine with the conception of *liang-chih*. Contrary to this view, Liang believes that the notion

of "extending *liang-chih*" is a change of slogan but has the same content as "*chih-hsing ho-i*" (ibid., p. 28). So also Chang regards the former as expressing the same idea as the latter but "in a more direct way" (Chang, *Wang Yang-ming*, p. 39). However one approaches Wang's philosophy as a whole, his doctrine of the unity of knowledge and action must occupy a central place. A plausible explication of this doctrine independent of his conception of *liang-chih* and *hsin* should contribute not only to the general interpretation of his philosophy, but also to the development of a Confucian moral psychology.

Chapter 1

1. For a discussion of this notion of actuating force of moral knowledge, see my *Dimensions of Moral Creativity: Paradigms, Principles, and Ideals* (University Park: Pennsylvania State University Press, 1978), chap. 2. This distinction in some way parallels Austin's distinction between meaning and force of speech-acts. (See J. L. Austin, *How to Do Things with Words*, p. 100.)

2. I adopt this term "aretaic" from W. K. Frankena's *Ethics* (Englewood Cliffs: Prentice-Hall, 1973), p. 9. But for the Confucian, the aretaic notion of *li*, for example, can be expressed in rulelike or quasi-denotic terms. *Li* may thus be rendered as "ritual rules." The important point to observe is that these aretaic notions or notions of virtue are all related to the moral ideal of human excellence. For the Confucian, this is the ideal of *jen* (in its general meaning) or *tao*. For a sustained treatment of the view that aretaic notions constitute an independent dimension of morality, see the discussion of "euergetical concepts" in Hector-Neri Castañeda, *The Structure of Morality* (Springfield: Charles C. Thomas, 1974), chap. 8; and French, *Scope of Morality*, chap. 7.

3. See, for example, *Analects* 4:16 and 6:28.

4. Thus Wang sometimes focuses on the unity of moral learning and action, a specific version of his doctrine of unity of moral knowledge and action, and sometimes on the creative aspect of learning (*Instructions*, sec. 115). For his critical attitude toward conventions, see particularly *Letters*, pp. 34, 42–43, 71.

5. Wing-tsit Chan (trans.), *A Source Book in Chinese Philosophy* (Princeton: Princeton University Press, 1963), p. 89. For an attempt to deal with a similar problem in classical Taoism, see my "Opposites as Complements: Reflections on the Significance of *Tao*," *Philosophy East and West*, vol. 31, no. 2 (1981).

6. Compare Ching, *To Acquire Wisdom*, p. 66.

7. For this distinction between ideal norm and ideal theme, see my *Dimension of Moral Creativity*, chap. 8.

8. *Letters*, p. 107. See also *Instructions*, sec. 291. This is Wang's consistent attitude toward dichotomies as noted by Nivison. See David Nivison, "The Problem of 'Knowledge' and 'Action' in Chinese Thought Since Wang Yang-ming," in Arthur F. Wright (ed.), *Studies in Chinese Thought* (Chicago: University of Chicago Press, 1953), p. 114.

9. "Inquiry on the *Great Learning*," in Chan, *Instructions*, p. 276.* In commenting on mind and *li* * ("principle"), Wang remarked that "the mind is the nature of man and things, and nature is *li* *. I am afraid the use of the word 'and' makes inevitable the interpretation of mind and principle as two different things. It is up to the student to use his good judgment." See *Instructions*, sec. 33. Query: Might the use of conjunction sometimes mislead us as to their intimate connection?

10. Unless indicated otherwise, the citations in this chapter are all taken from sec. 5 of *Instructions*. (The italics, other than the title and work in this instance, are mine.)

11. I do not deny at this point that in light of his doctrine of mind and *liang-chih* (innate knowledge of the good), it is possible, though not evidently plausible, to hold that Wang has in mind a sort of phenomenology of value perception. I have followed a different tack, admittedly an interpretation. The passage itself, independent of Wang's other conception, seems amenable to my treatment. I thus suspend my judgment on the thesis that Wang assimilates "our evaluating, and so our choosing, deciding and acting, to the notion of sense perception." See D. Nivison, "Moral Decision in Wang Yang-ming: The Problems of Chinese 'Existentialism,'" *Philosophy East and West*, vol. 23, nos. 1–2 (1973), p. 131.

12. For this distinction, see Austin, *Philosophical Papers*, p. 147.

13. Ludwig Wittgenstein, *Philosophical Investigations*, 3rd ed. (New York: Macmillan, 1969), pt. 2, pp. 197, 206, and 211.

14. For Wittgenstein's discussion of aspect blindness, see *Philosophical Investigations*, pt. 2, pp. 213–214.

15. According to Russell, "We have *acquaintance* with anything of which we are directly aware, without the intermediary of any process or inference or any knowledge of truths." See Bertrand Russell, *Problems of Philosophy* (Oxford: Oxford University Press, 1950), p. 46.

16. It is interesting to note that *Webster's Third New International Dictionary* contains an entry of obsolete sense of "knowledge" as "acknowledging" or "cognizance."

17. For a further discussion of this point, see my "Tasks of Confucian Ethics," *Journal of Chinese Philosophy*, vol. 6, no. 1 (1979), pp. 59–61.

18. In "Conscience and Moral Convictions," Ryle proposes the notion of
operative as distinct from *academic* knowledge—that is, in the sense of
"the knowledge or conviction which manifests itself in a disposition to behave." See 'lbert Ryle, *Collected Papers, 1929–1968*, vol. 2 (London:
Hutchinson & Co., 1971), p. 187. It is interesting to note that this notion of
operative knowledge seems akin to Aristotle's. In *Magna Moralia* (1201b),
Aristotle points out that there are two ways of knowing, "one of which is
the possessing knowledge, the other is putting the knowledge into operation. He who then possesses the knowledge of right but does not operate
with it is incontinent. When, then, he does not operate with this knowledge, it is nothing surprising that he should do what is bad, though he possesses the knowledge. For the case is the same as that of sleepers." On this
issue of incontinent man, Wang would differ in focusing on inoperative
knowledge not as a case of knowledge being "asleep," but rather in the self-
conscious regard for selfish desires. This moves the explanation of bad actions in terms that relate to a more conscious psychological feature of
moral agency.

19. See my *Dimensions of Moral Creativity*, pp. 28–34.

20. *Instructions*, sec. 211. Prospective moral knowledge may be shallow
compared to the retrospective sort. Nevertheless, it is a necessary prelude
to the latter.

21. *Instructions*, sec. 213.

22. For a suggestive remark of Wang, see *Instructions*, sec. 291.

23. As Murdoch points out, "Knowledge of a value concept is something
to be understood, as it were, in depth, and not in terms of switching on to
some impersonal network." See Iris Murdoch, *The Sovereignty of Good*
(London: Routledge & Kegan Paul, 1970), p. 29. See also my "Tasks of Confucian Ethics."

24. Tu, *Neo-Confucian Thought in Action*, p. 151.

25. We are still dealing with *Instructions*, sec. 5.

26. See Cheng, "Unity and Creativity," p. 60.

27. Wang Fu-chih justly remarked that what Wang Yang-ming "called
knowledge was not knowledge and what [he] called action not action," but
he failed to note that the unity of prospective and retrospective knowledge
is mediated by actual performance. Wang's doctrine may also be regarded
as an attempt to develop Confucius' stress on harmony of words *(yen)* and
deeds. For the former point, see Ian McMorran, "Late Ming Criticism of
Wang Yang-ming: The Case of Wang Fu-chih," *Philosophy East and West*,
vol. 23, nos. 1–2 (1973), p. 92; for the latter, see my *Dimensions of Moral
Creativity*, pp. 71–72, and "Reasonable Action and Confucian Argumentation," *Journal of Chinese Philosophy*, vol. 1, no. 1 (1973).

Chapter 2

1. *Instructions*, sec. 134. See also sec. 6.

2. *Instructions*, sec. 136*. Here I render *hsing* as doing rather than action proper. This is an emendation to make Wang's doctrine consistent. Doing is an activity, and this activity need not eventuate in moral performance. The present passage brings out another instance of the ambiguity of *hsing*, much akin to the one we noted between mere reflexive response and action in this essay [1.7]. But it is clear that here the doing is a *concerned* doing, which is Wang's focus on the basis or point of departure *(t'ou nao)*. See, for example, *Instructions*, sec. 2, and *Letters*, pp. 106–107.

3. As Rescher points out, "Every action must have an overt physical component and involves bodily activity of some sort." See Nicholas Rescher, "On the Characterization of Actions," in Myles Brand (ed.), *The Nature of Human Action* (Glenview: Scott, Foresman & Co., 1970), p. 248.

4. *Instructions*, sec. 144.

5. *Instructions*, sec. 6.

6. "Inquiry on the *Great Learning*" in *Instructions*, p. 279.

7. *Instructions*, sec. 6*. I replace Professor Chan's rendering of *tung* as "acting" by "moving," for *tung* seems to refer to bodily movement here rather than action.

8. See, for example, Ching, *To Acquire Wisdom*, entry of "intention" in the index.

9. Liang, *Wang Yang-ming chih-hsing ho-i chi chao*, pp. 11–12; Cheng, "Unity and Creativity," pp. 56–57.

10. *Instructions*, sec. 132.

11. *Instructions*, sec. 78.

12. Henke, *The Philosophy of Wang Yang-ming*, p. 463*. See also the same point stressed in a letter to his younger brother (ibid., pp. 469–471).

13. *Instructions*, sec. 71.

14. Thomas Reid, *Essays on the Active Powers of the Human Mind* (Cambridge: M.I.T. Press, 1969), pp. 58, 63.

15. But volition, arguably, is necessary to account for human action. See Lawrence H. Davis, *Theory of Action* (Englewood Cliffs: Prentice-Hall, 1979), chap. 1.

16. J. L. Austin, "Three Ways of Spilling Ink," in *Philosophical Papers*, p. 283.

17. See entry of "sincerity" in the index to *Instructions*.

18. *Instructions*, secs. 6 and 138.

19. Søren Kierkegaard, *Purity of Heart Is to Will One Thing* (New York: Harper & Row, 1965), p. 66.

20. *Instructions*, sec. 140. For Kierkegaard, see *Purity of Heart*, p. 56.

21. See, for instance, *Instructions*, sec. 2.

22. *Instructions*, sec. 132.

23. Harry Frankfurt, "Freedom of the Will and the Concept of a Person," *Journal of Philosophy*, vol. 68, no. 1 (1971), p. 10.

24. For an elaboration of responsible agency, see Charles Taylor, "What Is Human Agency?", in Theodore Mischel (ed.), *The Self: Psychological and Philosophical Issues* (Oxford: Basil Blackwell, 1977), or Charles Taylor, "Responsibility for Self," in Amelie Rorty (ed.), *The Identities of Persons* (Berkeley and Los Angeles: University of California Press, 1976).

25. See *Hsün Tzu, ch'eng-ming p'ien*. My translation differs from both H. H. Dubs and B. Watson. For a discussion of this difficult passage, see my "Dimensions of *Li* (Propriety)," pp. 380–381.

26. As one scholar points out, if it is seriously maintained that action is identical with knowledge, "a student will only seek his original mind and consequently neglect the *li** of things, and there will be points at which his mind will be closed to the outside world and unable to penetrate it." See *Instructions*, sec. 133.

27. *Instructions*, sec. 133.

28. This explanation is actually given in *Letters*, p. 106. As to retrospective knowledge, this is quite evident in Wang's use of *chen-chih* ("true knowledge") in his remark that "true knowledge is what constitutes action and that unless it is acted on it cannot be called knowledge." See *Instructions*, sec. 133; also *Instructions*, sec. 5.

29. *Instructions*, sec. 78.

30. *Instructions*, sec. 118*. The translation is Chan's except the first sentence, which is a literary rendering for the purpose of explication.

31. The theme is discussed in Chapter 4 [4.5–4.11].

32. *Instructions*, sec. 166.

33. *Instructions*, sec. 292.

34. *Instructions*, sec. 118.

35. This theme is extensively discussed in Chapter 4 [4.5–4.11].

36. It is interesting to compare this view with Ryle's: " 'Know' is a capacity verb of that special sort that is used for signifying that the persons described can bring things off or get things right." See Gilbert Ryle, *Concept of Mind* (New York: Barnes & Noble, 1949), p. 133.

37. See W. T. Chan, "The Evolution of Neo-Confucian *Li* as Principle," *Tsing Hua Journal of Chinese Studies*, NS 4, no. 2 (1964).

38. As I see it, the only way to render *li** as a "descriptive" notion is by taking seriously Kovesi's notion of "evaluative redescription." See J. Kovesi, "Against the Ritual of 'Is' and 'Ought,' " *Midwest Studies in Philosophy* (Studies in Ethical Theory), vol. 3 (Morris: University of Minnesota Press,

1978); see also J. Kovesi, *Moral Notions* (London: Routledge & Kegan Paul, 1967). See also my "Chinese Moral Vision, Responsive Agency, and Factual Beliefs," *Journal of Chinese Philosophy*, vol. 7, no. 1 (1980). Compare Chan, "The Evolution of Neo-Confucian *Li* as Principle," p. 139; and A. C. Graham, *Two Chinese Philosophers: Ch'eng Ming-tao and Ch'eng Yi-ch'uan* (London: Lund Humphries, 1958), p. 29.

39. For an incisive study, see Henry David Aiken, "On the Concept of a Moral Principle," in Carl G. Hemple et al., *Isenberg Memorial Lecture Series, 1965–1966* (East Lansing: Michigan State University Press, 1969).

40. This same procedure is employed in dealing with the homophone *li* ("ritual propriety") in my "Dimensions of *Li* (Propriety)," p. 375.

41. See *ch'eng ming p'ien*, in *Hsün Tzu*.

42. *Instructions*, sec. 3*.

43. *Instructions*, sec. 64.

44. See, for example, *Instructions*, secs. 76 and 96.

45. *Instructions*, sec. 3.

46. *Instructions*, sec. 4.

47. "Inquiry on the *Great Learning*" in *Instructions*, p. 272*.

48. The point regarding the analogy between two senses of seeing owes to the incisive essay of Norman Richard, "On Seeing Things Differently," *Radical Philosophy*, vol. 1, no. 1 (1972), reprinted in Rodger Beehler and Alan R. Drengson (eds.), *The Philosophy of Society* (London: Methuen, 1978), p. 318. But as Richard observes, the analogy does break down, for in the visual case, unlike the moral one—say, in Wittgenstein's duck-rabbit picture—when one becomes aware that it can be seen as a duck or as a rabbit, "nothing more can be said." "This is just where the case of conflicting moral perspectives is different. One can see a thing in two different ways without feeling this as a tension, but one cannot live on the basis of two incompatible moral perspectives. . . . This is what constitutes the real importance of the notion of 'commitment' and 'choice' in ethics." (Ibid., p. 336.) Recall our discussion of *yi* as will [2.3].

49. *Instructions*, sec. 133.

50. I do not pursue here the question of whether such a function of *li** is acceptable for a theory of moral justification. This question presupposes that one has an adequate theory of moral justification. When justification is construed in terms of the agent's vindication of his conduct in response to the challenge about its rightness, the Confucian view may be rendered plausible. For an attempt in this direction inspired by both John Searle and the classical Confucian doctrine of rectifying terms, see my "Reasonable Action and Confucian Argumentation," *Journal of Chinese Philosophy*, vol. 1, no. 1 (1973).

51. *Instructions*, sec. 52*. This emendation is not intended to improve

Professor Chan's felicitous translation. In fact it is more literary and wordy, but the emendation, if correct, serves better as a basis for my explication of *tao-li**. In terms of its stress on the sense of timing, this passage has a striking affinity to a statement of the Neo-Taoist Kuo Hsiang: "Humanity *(jen)* and righteousness *(i)* belong to human nature. Human nature undergoes changes and is different past and present. If one takes a temporary abode in a thing and then moves on, he will silently understand [the reality of things]. If, however, he stops and is confined to one place, he will develop prejudices. Prejudices will result in hypocrisy, and hypocrisy will result in many reproaches." See Chan, *Source Book in Chinese Philosophy*, p. 335.

52. *Instructions*, sec. 66. For similar emphasis see *Letters*, p. 29.

53. This is, in Geach's sense, an attributive rather than a predicative adjective. Although "*x* is a red book" can be logically split into "*x* is a book" and "*x* is red," we cannot split "*x* is a *tao-li**" into "*x* is *tao*" and "*x* is *li**." See Peter Geach, "Good and Evil," *Analysis*, vol. 17 (1956), reprinted in Philippa Foot (ed.), *Theories of Ethics* (Oxford: Oxford University Press, 1967), p. 64.

54. Aiken, "On the Concept of a Moral Principle," p. 113. My former appropriation of Kovesi's similar insight appears in *Dimensions of Moral Creativity*, p. 81. For Kovesi's discussion, see his *Moral Notions*, p. 93f.

55. *Instructions*, sec. 340.

56. *Instructions*, sec. 177. See also *Letters*, p. 76.

57. See my *Dimensions of Moral Creativity*, pp. 40–44, and "Some Responses to Criticisms," *Journal of Chinese Philosophy*, vol. 7, no. 1 (1980).

58. *Instructions*, sec. 276.

59. Ibid. This passage raises at least two difficult issues that I cannot pursue here. For one thing, the focus on human relationships *(lun)* may appear problematic without accommodating the notion of rights of the persons involved. I have dealt with this issue in "*Li* and Moral Justification." There is also a question of the plausible response of a Confucian to the problem of moral conflict and the role of *li* or ritual propriety. The complexity of the latter is discussed in my "Dimensions of *Li* (Propriety)." To my knowledge, the former does not appear to admit of unequivocal answer, and this in part pertains to the aretaic notions as open rather than complete moral notions in Kovesi's sense (*Moral Notions*, p. 109). What I have to say now on this latter issue is intended to provide a beginning for a fuller treatment. My remarks on this perplexing passage are thus tentative in spirit and not to be taken as a Confucian contribution to the problem of moral justification.

60. D. C. Lau (trans.), *Mencius* (Baltimore: Penguin Books, 1970), 7A: 46*. See also *Mencius* 6A:10 and 6A:14.

61. For a discussion of this conception of ideal theme as an action-guide, see my "Some Responses to Criticisms," *Journal of Chinese Philosophy*, vol. 7, no. 1 (1980).

62. I am most grateful to Professor Paul Weiss for his critique of my Confucian view in response to my query on his recent incisive book. Some of the remarks that follow are excerpted from our correspondence, but they are to be taken as my groping toward a more adequate formulation of the Confucian view. The quotation is taken from *You, I, and the Others* (Carbondale: Southern Illinois University Press, 1980), p. 84.

63. *Mencius* 4A:10.

64. For a detailed discussion of this notion of vindication of actions, see my "Reasonable Action and Confucian Argumentation" and "Uses of Dialogues and Moral Understanding," *Journal of Chinese Philosophy*, vol. 2, no. 2 (1975).

65. My exposition is based on Wang's explanation of his vision of *jen* that the great man "forms one body" with Heaven, Earth, and all things. A partial quotation is revealing: "When he observes the pitiful cries and frightened appearance of birds and animals about to be slaughtered, he cannot help feeling an 'inability to bear' their suffering. This shows that his humanity *(jen)* forms one body with birds and animals. It may be objected that birds and animals are sentient beings as he is. But when he sees plants broken and destroyed, he cannot help a feeling of pity. It may be said that plants are living things as he is. Yet, even when he sees tiles and stones shattered and crushed, he cannot help a feeling of regret. This shows that his humanity forms one body with tiles and stones." See *Instructions*, p. 272.

66. The expression "remorse without repudiation" owes to D. Z. Phillips and H. O. Mounce, *Moral Practices*, p. 101.

67. See *Analects* 1:2.

68. Melden, *Rights and Persons*, p. 153.

69. *Instructions*, sec. 115.

70. See *tzu-tao p'ien* in *Hsün Tzu*.

71. This sentence is a paraphrase and not a translation from Hsün Tzu's *pou-kou p'ien* and *chih-shih p'ien*. For a detailed discussion of relevant passages in *Li Chi*, see my "*Li* and Moral Justification."

72. *Instructions*, sec. 281.

73. *Instructions*, sec. 22.

74. *Instructions*, sec. 141.

75. "The highest good is none other than the mind's complete embodiment of *t'ien-li**." See *Instructions*, sec. 4*. On this relatively unexplored topic of transformation of classical idioms in Neo-Confucianism, Professor Cheng aptly points out that "the main issue in Sung-Ming Neo-Confucianism seems to be one of relating the latter-day concept of *li** to classical

idioms of moral psychology, moral metaphysics and morality, not only for the purpose of unraveling the deeper meanings of *li** as a concept, but for the purpose of retrieving and developing the logical implications of classical idioms in a new light." It is hoped that my present discussion of *li** provides a small beginning to this larger task. See Chung-ying Cheng, "Consistency and Meaning of the Four-Sentence Teaching in *Ming Ju Hsüeh An*," *Philosophy East and West*, vol. 29, no. 3 (1979), p. 276.

76. *Letters*, pp. 29–30*.

77. Aristotle, *Nicomachean Ethics*, trans. Martin Ostwald (Indianapolis: Bobbs-Merrill, 1962), 1144b. For further discussion, see [4.17].

78. *Instructions*, sec. 133. See also *Instructions*, secs. 153 and 276.

79. Bernard Karlgren, *Analytic Dictionary of Chinese and Sino-Japanese* (Taipei: Ch'eng-Wen Publishing Co., 1975).

80. To forestall misunderstanding, I do not equate *li** as organic unity with Moore's notion of intrinsic goods, though I have appropriated the term from his discussion. As expressive of organic unity, the notion of *li** suggests an affinity with Moore's conception of intrinsic goods as organic wholes. This comparison, however, is highly misleading. Wang was not an ideal utilitarian. His notion of moral thinking or reflection, as we shall see later [3.5], does not deal with causal consequences in terms of an aggregate of intrinsic goods. The notion of *li** basically pertains to the agent's integration of his inner states (thoughts, desires, and feelings, for example) and outward events. As organic wholes, Moore's personal relations and aesthetic experiences would be acceptable to Wang—not because they are intrinsically good in the sense that they "are judged to be good if they existed by themselves, in absolute isolation," but because they are judged to be eligible constituents of *tao* or *jen* experience. As a moral ideal, *jen* obviously concerns "the *best* state of things *conceivable*," but this notion is acknowledged by Moore to fall outside the scope of his investigation. Moore's notion of intrinsic good, moreover, cannot be properly applied to *tao* or *jen*. *Tao* or *jen* is not something that can exist in "absolute isolation" or something to be discovered by Moore's method of isolation for intrinsic goods. Unlike utilitarians, the Neo-Confucians did not propose any general formula for guiding and assessing moral conduct. This absence of a formula for right action marks a distinctive feature of both classical and Neo-Confucian ethics. In this respect, the concept of right action resembles that of the doctrine of perceptual intuitionism. In the case of Mencius, or more prominently that of Wang Yang-ming, there appears a form of intuitionism in their notion of *liang-chih*. But even in this case, *liang-chih* is more an innate capacity for moral discrimination than a principle of moral justification. For comparative purpose, perhaps the best course is to attend to Lewis's conception of the good life on the whole as a "temporal gestalt."

The notion of *li**** in the context of *jen* as a moral ideal suggests such a conception. Wang would probably accept, with some modification, Lewis's account. In this view, the value of a good life on the whole is "found to be realized in the living of it." The relation of good and bad experiences in "constituting a good or bad life is not that of a series of temporally juxtaposed and externally related moments but . . . that of ingredients which affect and qualify one another: the relations of components in a temporal *Gestalt*." This notion of the good life is a notion of dynamic organic unity that clearly contrasts with a static inclusivistic or aggregative conception. The moral agent's problem, for Wang, is the problem of creative constitution of the import of *jen* by way of thought and action [3.4]. For moral theory, this view obviously rests on an assumption of the internal relations between the means and the end—an assumption that requires further examination. For the present, let us merely contend with a suggestion that an analysis of this Neo-Confucian problem can benefit from a study of this aspect of Lewis's theory of value. See Moore, *Principia Ethica*, pp. 25, 183–187; and C. I. Lewis, *An Analysis of Knowledge and Valuation* (La Salle: Open Court, 1946), p. 486.

81. Joseph Needham, *Science and Civilization in China*, vol. 2: *History of Scientific Thought* (Cambridge: Cambridge University Press, 1962), p. 567.

82. *Instructions*, sec. 222***. I find it difficult to make sense out of this passage without an interpolation. The interpretation to follow is suggested in Wang's complaint against the fragmentary character of scholars who, as Wang says, "adhere to added commentaries and do not investigate deeply the meaning [significance] of the Classics." "These scholars, stopping at the literal understanding of words, do not pay attention to the direct experience of their mind and person. That is why [their] knowledge becomes fragmentary, and they achieve nothing in the end." See *Letters*, p. 39; see also *Letters*, pp. 67, 70–71, 74; and *Instructions*, secs. 130, 137, 143; and "Inquiry on the *Great Learning*" in *Instructions*, p. 274.

83. W. D. Ross, *The Right and the Good* (Oxford: Clarendon Press, 1930), p. 28. In using this notion of toti-resultant attribute, I do not mean to suggest that Confucian aretaic notions refer to prima facie duties, though they can be so treated. At issue, however, is not Ross's notion of the tendency of a duty to be an actual duty, but rather the exercise of judgment in accordance with a sense of what is right.

84. *Instructions*, sec. 322.

85. This explication quite naturally gives rise to the question of whether Wang can go on, as he does, in connecting *li**** and mind in some universal and comprehensive way suggestive of a form of ontological idealism. This question is pursued in Chapter 4 [4.5–4.11].

86. *Instructions*, sec. 9*. See also Wang's preface to the *Li Chih* in Ching, *To Acquire Wisdom*, p. 202. The connection between *li** and *li* (propriety) is actually explicit in two passages in the *Li Chih*. In so doing, all ritual performances—mourning, sacrifices, rites of passage, and so forth —may be regarded as examples of occasional achievement of temporal order. See James Legge (trans.), *The Li Chih or Collection of Treatises on the Rules of Propriety and Ceremonial Usages* (Delhi: Motilal Barnarsidaas, 1966), vol. 2, pp. 271, 275. For a detailed examination of the connection between *li* and moral justification, see my "*Li* and Moral Justification."

87. *Instructions*, sec. 9.

88. For a detailed account, see my "Dimensions of *Li* (Propriety)."

89. *Letters*, p. 107. See also *Instructions*, sec. 291.

90. Graham, *Two Chinese Philosophers*, p. 18.

91. "The human mind and *t'ien-li** are undifferentiated. Sages and worthies wrote about them very much like a portrait painter painting the true likeness and transmitting the spirit. He shows only an outline of the appearance to serve as a basis for the people to seek and find their true personality. Among one's spirit, feelings, and behavior, there is that which cannot be transmitted. Later writers have imitated and copied what the sages have drawn. They have erroneously mutilated it and have added to it in their own way in order to show off their own tricks. In this way the original is further and further lost." See *Instructions*, sec. 20.

Chapter 3

1. For this notion of root metaphor, see S. C. Pepper, *World Hypotheses* (Berkeley and Los Angeles: University of California Press, 1948), chap. 5.

2. Chan, *Source Book in Chinese Philosophy*, p. 550.

3. Ibid. For a study of this Confucian classic, see my "Confucian Vision and Experience of the World," *Philosophy East and West*, vol. 25, no. 3 (1975).

4. See Cheng Chung-ying, "Harmony and Conflict in Chinese Philosophy," *Journal of Chinese Philosophy*, vol. 4, no. 3 (1977).

5. *Instructions*, sec. 115.

6. Aristotle, *Nichomachean Ethics*, 1174b.

7. *Instructions*, sec. 45.

8. *Instructions*, sec. 120.

9. See Søren Kierkegaard, *Concluding Unscientific Postscript* (Princeton: Princeton University Press, 1941), pt. 2, chap. 2.

10. Chan, *Source Book in Chinese Philosophy*, p. 609.

11. Jaakko Hintikka, "Practical vs. Theoretical Reason—An Ambiguous

Legacy," in Stephen Körner (ed.), *Practical Reason* (New Haven: Yale University Press, 1974), p. 84.

12. Pepper, *World Hypotheses*, p. 256.

13. Stuart Hampshire, *Thought and Action*, p. 193. See also Brand Blanshard, *Reason and Goodness* (London: Allen & Unwin, 1961), pp. 303–305; and Andrew Harrison, "Creativity and Understanding," *Proceedings of the Aristotelean Society*, supp. vol. 41 (1971); and my *Dimensions of Moral Creativity*, p. 141.

14. *Instructions*, sec. 99.

15. Fung Yu-lan, *A History of Chinese Philosophy*, vol. 2 (Princeton: Princeton University Press, 1953), p. 215.

16. Although the words *chin-ssu* occur in the title of Chu Hsi and Lü Tsu-ch'ien's influential Neo-Confucian anthology, only two terse passages deal with this notion explicitly. The following explication is an incomplete reconstruction of this important notion largely inspired by Professor Chan's rendering in terms of "reflections of things at hand." See Wing-tsit Chan (trans.), *Reflections of Things at Hand: A Neo-Confucian Anthology of Chu Hsi and Lü Tsu-ch'ien* (New York: Columbia University Press, 1967).

17. *Instructions*, sec. 21. The use of the mirror metaphor in depicting the sage's mind is a favorite among Chinese philosophers. Chuang Tzu seems to have originated the use. For some of its occurrences, see the "mirror" entry in the index to Chan's *Source Book*. Brief discussions of Ch'eng Hao's use are found in Fung, *History of Chinese Philosophy*, vol. 2, pp. 525–526, and Graham, *Two Chinese Philosophers*, p. 105. To some extent, the common use of "still or clear water" serves much the same purpose. My choice here is based on convenience in illustrating a pervasive feature of Chinese moral thought. Even a relatively conservative moralist like Hsün Tzu has found a Confucian use of "clear water" in his discussion of sagehood. See B. Watson (trans.), *Hsün Tzu: Basic Writings* (New York: Columbia University Press, 1963), p. 131.

18. The following analysis is an appropriation, with modification, of Professor Matson's insightful discussion of what he calls "sizing up" activity. See W. Matson, *Sentience* (Berkeley and Los Angeles: University of California Press, 1976), chap. 5.

19. Matson, *Sentience*, p. 151.

20. Kovesi, *Moral Notions*, p. 119.

21. See S. C. Pepper, *Sources of Value* (Berkeley and Los Angeles: University of California Press, 1958), p. 437f.

22. For further discussion, see my "Practical Causation and Confucian Ethics," *Philosophy East and West*, vol. 25, no. 1 (1965).

23. Ching, *To Acquire Wisdom*, p. 66.

Chapter 4

1. *Instructions*, sec. 133.
2. *Letters*, p. 23.
3. Preface to *Instructions*, p. xix.
4. Tu, *Neo-Confucian Thought in Action*, p. 63.
5. Ibid., p. 175.
6. See, for example, *Instructions*, secs. 66, 76, 96, 119, 125, 172, 205, 211–213, 249, 280, 296.
7. *Instructions*, sec. 5. (Italics mine.)
8. Phillips and Mounce, *Moral Practices*, p. 87.
9. *Letters*, p. 82.
10. *Instructions*, sec. 106; see also secs. 226, 279. Note that this sort of regret is quite distinct from regret without repudiation discussed in the text [2.15].
11. Chan's comment on "The Community Compact for Southern Kanchou (1518)," *Instructions*, p. 298.
12. *Instructions*, p. 300. (Italics mine.)
13. *Instructions*, sec. 246.
14. Of course, the agent can form first-personal precepts as an aid to understanding the cognitive content of aretaic notions [2.13].
15. As Wiggens incisively points out, moral deliberation (or what I term moral reflection) is not a technical deliberation. In this nontechnical deliberation, "I shall characteristically have an extremely vague description of something I want—a good life, a satisfying profession, an interesting holiday, an amusing evening—and the problem is not to see what will be causally efficacious in bringing this about, but to see what really *qualifies* as an adequate and practically realizable specification of what would satisfy this want." See David Wiggens, "Deliberation and Practical Reason," *Proceedings of the Aristotelean Society*, 1975–1976, p. 38. See also D. C. Lau (trans.), *Mencius*, app. 5, pp. 245–246; Lewis, *Analysis of Knowledge and Valuation*, chap. 16.
16. Thus Wang sometimes expresses his doctrine in terms of the simultaneous pursuit of both knowing and doing. See, for example, *Instructions*, sec. 132.
17. *Instructions*, sec. 319. From this experience, Wang arrived at the conception of investigation of things *(ko-wu)* in the *Great Learning* as primarily a task to be prosecuted with reference to one's body and mind. This may appear to be a bizarre inversion of the pursuit of factual knowledge, but one must respect Wang's own experience and the insight that prospective moral knowledge cannot be sought for in factual investigation. How

one moves from it to retrospective knowledge, apart from moral reflection attentive to *li** of particular situations, is a matter of *yi*, of will, intention, and the second-order moral desire to attain the highest good [2.4–2.5]. And this insight is independent of the question of his misinterpretation of Chu Hsi's doctrine. It is interesting to note that the nature of Wang's experience has affinity to Tolstoy's main character, Ivan Ilych, who "discovered" the meaning of life on his death bed by acquiring a capacity to feel sorrow for those who bore the burden of his dying days. See Leo Tolstoy, *The Death of Ivan Ilych* (New York: New American Library, 1960).

18. See Stefan Zweig, "Transfiguration," in G. B. Levitas (ed.), *The World of Psychoanalysis*, vol. 2 (New York: George Braziller, 1965).

19. See my "Practical Causation and Confucian Ethics," pp. 6–8.

20. In sketchy form, the hypothesis on the language of vision has been given in my "Confucian Vision and Experience of the World." More elaboration on the relation between ideal theme and factual beliefs is offered in pt. 3 of "Chinese Moral Vision, Responsive Agency, and Factual Beliefs." Earlier, while struggling with the notion of *jen* in the *Analects*, I received great aid and inspiration from Wheelwright's discussion in *Burning Fountain* of plurisignations, a term which I adopted in my "Reflections on the Structure of Confucian Ethics," *Philosophy East and West*, vol. 21, no. 2 (1971), later incorporated with some revision in my *Dimensions of Moral Creativity*, chap. 4. I have also profited a great deal from Robert J. Fogelin's treatment of amphibious statements in *Evidence and Meaning* (London: Routledge & Kegan Paul, 1967) and Karl Aschenbrenner's notion of characterization in *The Concepts of Value* (Dordrecht: D. Reidel, 1971). My use of what I call "amphibious notions" and "characterization" cannot be ascribed to Fogelin and Aschenbrenner, however, though I am obviously indebted to their discussions of these notions. My exposition should be evaluated as an independent attempt at explicating the language of Confucian vision utilizing what I regard as the insights of these philosophers for formulating a coherent hypothesis concerning the language of vision. My hypothesis is highly tentative. I have attempted no more than an informal presentation, for I am uncertain about the utility of precision for explicating the Confucian language of vision. I have therefore made no claim to presenting a general theory. I should be content if my present discussion serves as a stimulus for others who are interested in the language of moral vision. Regarding classical Taoism, I have followed a somewhat different approach in "Opposites as Complements: Reflections on the Significance of *Tao*." Related to this study is my "Forgetting Morality: Reflections on a Theme in *Chuang Tzu*," *Journal of Chinese Philosophy*, vol. 4, no. 4 (1977).

21. This and the following two paragraphs incorporate with revision what I wrote in "Chinese Moral Vision, Responsive Agency, and Factual Beliefs," pp. 18–19.

22. Aschenbrenner uses the term "characterization" for "sentences whose principal purpose . . . is to appraise, judge or evaluate." And "to characterize is to survey the properties and behavior of a thing or a person, or even a part or aspect of these, not simply to report them but to 'sum up' the subject in a unique way." See *The Concepts of Value*, pp. 117. I appropriated this notion for the language of vision rather than persons as the subjects of appraisal. Further, the vision so characterized does not have a compendious function except as a unifying perspective for viewing the actuating import of any survey of the properties and behavior of things and persons.

23. *Instructions*, secs. 177 and 172.

24. For an extensive discussion of Confucian discourse and argumentation, see my "Reasonable Action and Confucian Argumentation" and "Uses of Dialogues and Moral Understanding." When *li** is deployed in ordinary Confucian discourse, our discussion of *li** as reason in Chapter 2 is likely to apply. A focus on the appeal to the *li**, say, of filiality is a reason-giving appeal or appeal to *reasonableness*. It is interesting to explore further how the Neo-Confucian *li** can be systematically treated as an important argumentative factor in Confucian discourse.

25. The term "constitutive means" as distinct from "instrumental means" is proposed in D. C. Lau, "On Mencius' Use of Analogy in Arguments" (Lau, *Mencius*, pp. 245–246). This is a better term than the standard "contributory goods," introduced and extensively discussed in Lewis, *Analysis of Knowledge and Valuation*, chap. 16.

26. Fogelin, *Evidence and Meaning*, p. 42.

27. *Instructions*, sec. 66*.

28. Ruth Saw, *Aesthetics* (New York: Anchor Books, 1971), p. 197.

29. I do not deny but simply lay aside the obvious possibility that amphibious notions can also be construed as "proto-metaphysical notions" or root metaphors in Pepper's sense. This possibility, I believe, is germane to those who claim that Wang has a moral metaphysics. Embarking upon the exploration of this important topic would take us far beyond the scope of this study. It must be acknowledged that I learned a great deal in a recent discussion of this topic on the Confucian language of vision with Cheng Chung-ying—in particular, the way in which amphibious notions function as ampliative notions.

30. *Instructions*, sec. 66; *Letters*, p. 102.

31. *Instructions*, sec. 10.

32. *Instructions*, sec. 174; "Preface to Li Chi" in Ching, *To Acquire Wisdom*, p. 202.

33. See note 29 of this chapter.

34. Dorothy Emmet, *The Moral Prism* (London: Macmillan, 1979), p. 138. In many ways this book gives an emphasis to the distinction between A-type and B-type teleology—a distinction which closely parallels my own distinction between ideal theme and ideal norm discussed in *Dimensions of Moral Creativity* (chap. 8). For an appreciative but critical response, see my review of Emmet's book in *Philosophical Books*, vol. 21, no. 4 (1980). For an emphasis on transcendental terms similar to Emmet's, see Iris Murdoch, *Sovereignty of Good*.

35. *Instructions*, sec. 66.

36. These four expressions are found in *Instructions*, secs. 66, 31, 3, 9 (and Ching, *To Acquire Wisdom*, p. 202). The expression "mind *(hsin)* is *(chi) li*'" is found in many places, and there is certainly ground, as most scholars agree, to take this as a key expression for unlocking Wang's philosophy of mind and metaphysics. See, for example, Cheng's "Unity and Creativity" and Ching, *To Acquire Wisdom*, chap. 2. Quite deliberately I omitted such expressions as "*liang-chih* is *(chi-shih) tao*" (*Instructions*, sec. 165), for this would involve us in Wang's peculiar version, not presently clear to me, of ethical intuitionism.

37. Ching, *To Acquire Wisdom*, p. 57*.

38. Austin, *Philosophical Papers*, pp. 69–75.

39. As Chan points out, "To consider principles *(li*)* as external [is] an idea entirely unacceptable to Wang" (*Instructions*, p. xxxi); for relevant passages see secs. 135, 173, 201.

40. *Instructions*, sec. 49; the same notion of "one thread" appears in a passage on extending *liang-chih* in sec. 140.

41. Wheelwright, *Burning Fountain*, p. 81.

42. For a discussion of the uses of the notion of intuition and their arguments, see the appendix to my *Reason and Virtue: A Study in the Ethics of Richard Price* (Athens: Ohio University Press, 1966).

43. William James, *Essays in Radical Empiricism and a Pluralistic Universe* (New York: E. P. Dutton, 1971), p. 131.

44. *Instructions*, sec. 176. In another letter, Wang writes, "The learning of the sages of the past and the present is the public property of the whole world and not a private property of the three of us" (*Letters*, p. 76).

45. There is an initial problem with respect to the question of evaluation. Although as Fang points out there is an axiological unity in Wang's philosophy as a whole, the absence of any conception of hierarchy of values [2.15] poses a difficult task for comparative evaluation. Unless one is

to espouse a version of axiological monism, there is doubt whether comparative evaluation can properly be attempted—particularly for Wang's Confucian vision, which stresses personal realization or experience as the ultimate test for the adequacy of his vision [4.1]. At issue is the possibility of evaluating moral visions. It has been argued incisively that the very nature of the vision itself forecloses the intelligibility of rational evaluation, although adoption of the vision need not be a mere matter of personal taste. But to this insight we need to add that an inquiry into the possibility of discovering common features between moral visions is important. If there are such features, or functionally equivalent ones, we have some ground for objective evaluation. For if it is reasonable to adopt one vision, it is also reasonable to adopt the functionally equivalent one. In this way, one vision, though focusing on experience, need not preclude its being a reasonable one. Thus it is an essential preliminary to map out conditions of reasonableness that appear implicit in the explication of a moral vision before raising the large axiological question of comparative evaluation. This is part of the procedure I follow in concluding this study. See Thomé H. Fang, "The Essence of Wang Yang-ming's Philosophy," *Philosophy East and West*, vol. 23, nos. 1–2 (1973), p. 73; Richard, "On Seeing Things Differently."

46. This distinction owes to the incisive essay of Herbert Feigl, "Validation and Vindication," in Wilfred Sellars and John Hospers (eds.), *Readings in Ethical Theory* (New York: Appleton-Century-Crofts, 1952). It must be noted that vindication is also quite properly used with respect to an agent's justifying his conduct when he is challenged by fellow agents. This is the notion employed in my "Reasonable Action and Confucian Argumentation."

47. Richard, "On Seeing Things Differently," p. 337.

48. *Instructions*, sec. 205. See also secs. 166 and 292.

49. Chaim Perelman, "The Rational and the Reasonable," *The New Rhetoric and the Humanities: Essays on Rhetoric and Its Applications* (Dordrecht: D. Reidel, 1979), p. 117.

50. Aristotle, *Nicomachean Ethics*, 1140a.

51. I have profited much in reading some recent discussions of the significance of the notion of reasonableness. The literature that attends exclusively to this topic, to my knowledge, is not extensive. Readers may wish to compare my discussion with the following: John Rawls, "Outline of a Decision Procedure for Ethics," *Philosophical Review*, vol. 60, no. 2 (1951); W. H. Sibley, "The Rational vs. the Reasonable," *Philosophical Review*, vol. 62, no. 4 (1953); Nicholas Rescher, "Reasoned Justification of Moral Judgments," *Journal of Philosophy*, vol. 55, no. 6 (1958); William Dennis,

"An Appeal to Reason," in *Reason,* University of California Publications in Philosophy, vol. 27 (Berkeley: University of California Press, 1939), and "Conflict," in Sidney Hook (ed.), *American Philosophers at Work* (New York: Criterion Books, 1956); Kai Nielsen, "Appealing to Reason," *Inquiry,* vol. 1 (1962); J. R. Lucas, "The Philosophy of the Reasonable Man," *Philosophical Quarterly,* vol. 13, no. 51 (1963); and Perelman, cited in Note 49. For my own account, in part indebted to Perelman's earlier work, on the notion of reasonable judgment and action, see *Dimensions of Moral Creativity,* pp. 92–98. Unlike Dennis and Nielsen, I do not include the uses of reason in science, logic and mathematics, and conceptual analysis, for these seem too stringent a requirement for being reasonable. This view implies that reasonableness should be subsumed under some larger notion of rationality. Further, I do not follow Nielsen in including "principle of reasonable behavior" to the effect that to reason in (his) sense is to reason in accordance with the following rule: "For any *x* and for any *A,* if *x* desires *A* and if *x* is not willing to make *A* a universal imperative, then *x* ought *not* to do *A,* even though *x* wants to do *A*" (Nielsen, "Appealing to Reason," p. 69). This Kantian requirement of universalizability is more a requirement for rational rather than reasonable moral behavior. Of course, one can always collapse the distinction between rationality and reasonableness by philosophical legislation. But if the distinction is in order, as Lucas points out, there is "the social structure of reasonableness" which cannot be reduced to tidy rules for judgment (Lucas, "Philosophy of Reasonable Man," p. 98).

52. *Analects* 18:8 (Legge's translation). For further discussion of this theme in Confucius and Mencius, see my *Dimensions of Moral Creativity,* pp. 69–76.

53. *Instructions,* sec. 121.

54. *Letters,* p. 70.

55. This feature is stressed in Dennis's discussion. See Dennis, "Conflict," p. 338.

56. *Analects* 1:2, 4:15, 5:11, 6:28, 12:2; *Instructions,* sec. 93 and pp. 273–274.

57. *Analects* 6:28; see Chan, *Source Book in Chinese Philosophy,* p. 31*.

58. This point is suggested in Hsün Tzu's essay "Against Physiognomy" *[Fei-hsiang p'ien].* See Dubs, *Works of Hsüntze,* p. 74. For a more extensive discussion of the notion of Confucian concern for others, see my "Confucian Vision and Human Community," presented at the Conference on Society and Unity, International Society for Metaphysics, King's College, London, 21 July 1980. For an incisive contemporary treatment of the Golden Rule, see Marcus Singer, "Golden Rule," *Philosophy,* vol. 63 (1963).

59. *Analects* 19:6.

60. *Letters*, p. 34.

61. *Letters*, p. 63; see also *Letters*, p. 71.

62. *Instructions*, sec. 304.

63. *Doctrine of the Mean*, sec. 6; Chan, *Source Book in Chinese Philosophy*, p. 99.

64. *Instructions*, sec. 45.

65. Aristotle, *Nicomachean Ethics*, 1104a.

Bibliography

Aiken, Henry D. "On the Concept of a Moral Principle." In Carl Hempel et al., *The Isenberg Memorial Lecture Series, 1965–1966*. East Lansing: Michigan State University Press, 1969.

Anscombe, G.E.M. "Modern Moral Philosophy." In *The Definition of Morality*, edited by G. Wallace and A.D.M. Walker. London: Methuen, 1970.

Aristotle, *Magna Moralia*. Translated by St. George Stock. In *The Works of Aristotle*. Vol. 9. Oxford: Oxford University Press, 1954.

———. *Nicomachean Ethics*. Translated by Martin Ostwald. Indianapolis: Bobbs-Merrill, 1962.

Aschenbrenner, Karl. *The Concepts of Value*. Dordrecht: D. Reidel, 1971.

Austin, J. L. *Philosophical Papers*. 2nd ed. Oxford: Clarendon Press, 1961.

———. *How to Do Things with Words*. Cambridge: Harvard University Press, 1962.

Beehler, Rodger and Drengsen, Alan R. Editors. *The Philosophy of Society*. London: Methuen, 1978.

Blanshard, Brand. *Reason and Goodness*. London: Allen & Unwin, 1961.

Brandt, Richard. *A Theory of the Good and the Right*. New York: Oxford University Press, 1979.

Castañeda, Hector-Neri. *The Structure of Morality*. Springfield: Charles C Thomas, 1974.

Chan, Wing-tsit. Translator. *A Source Book in Chinese Philosophy*. Princeton: Princeton University Press, 1963.

———. Translator. *Instructions for Practical Living and Other Neo-Confucian Writings by Wang Yang-ming*. New York: Columbia University Press, 1963.

———. "The Evolution of Neo-Confucian *Li* as Principle." *Tsing Hua Journal of Chinese Studies*, NS 4, no. 2 (1964).

_____. Translator. *Reflections of Things at Hand: A Neo-Confucian Anthology of Chu Hsi and Lü Tsu-ch'ien.* New York: Columbia University Press, 1967.

Chang, Carsun. *Wang Yang-ming: Idealist Philosopher of Sixteenth-Century China.* Jamaica: St. John's University Press, 1962.

Cheng, Chung-ying. "Unity and Creativity in Wang Yang-ming's Philosophy of Mind." *Philosophy East and West,* vol. 23, nos. 2–3 (1973).

_____. "Harmony and Conflict in Chinese Philosophy." *Journal of Chinese Philosophy,* vol. 4, no. 3 (1977).

_____. "Consistency and Meaning of the Four-Sentence Teaching in *Ming Ju Hsüeh An.*" *Philosophy East and West,* vol. 29, no. 3 (1979).

Ching, Julia. Translator. *The Philosophical Letters of Wang Yang-ming.* Columbia: University of South Carolina Press, 1972.

_____. *To Acquire Wisdom: The Way of Wang Yang-ming.* New York: Columbia University Press, 1976.

Cua, A. S. *Reason and Virtue: A Study in the Ethics of Richard Price.* Athens: Ohio University Press, 1966.

_____. "Reasonable Action and Confucian Argumentation." *Journal of Chinese Philosophy,* vol. 1, no. 1 (1973).

_____. "Practical Causation and Confucian Ethics." *Philosophy East and West,* vol. 25, no. 1 (1975).

_____. "Confucian Vision and Experience of the World." *Philosophy East and West,* vol. 25, no. 3 (1975).

_____. "Uses of Dialogues and Moral Understanding." *Journal of Chinese Philosophy,* vol. 2, no. 2 (1975).

_____. "Forgetting Morality: Reflections on a Theme in *Chuang Tzu.*" *Journal of Chinese Philosophy,* vol. 4, no. 4 (1977).

_____. *Dimensions of Moral Creativity: Paradigms, Principles, and Ideals.* University Park: Pennsylvania State University Press, 1978.

_____. "Dimensions of *Li* (Propriety): Reflections on an Aspect of Hsün Tzu's Ethics." *Philosophy East and West,* vol. 29, no. 4 (1979).

_____. "Tasks of Confucian Ethics." *Journal of Chinese Philosophy,* vol. 6, no. 1 (1979).

_____. "Chinese Moral Vision, Responsive Agency, and Factual Beliefs." *Journal of Chinese Philosophy,* vol. 7, no. 1 (1980).

_____. "Some Responses to Criticisms." *Journal of Chinese Philosophy,* vol. 7, no. 1 (1980).

_____. "Opposites as Complements: Reflections on the Significance of *Tao.*" *Philosophy East and West,* vol. 31, no. 2 (1981).

_____. "*Li* and Moral Justification: A Study in the *Li Chi,*" *Philosophy East and West,* forthcoming.

———. "Confucian Vision and Human Community." In *Society and Unity*, edited by George McLean. Oxford: Oxford University Press, forthcoming.

Davis, Lawrence H. *Theory of Action*. Englewood Cliffs: Prentice-Hall, 1979.

Dennis, William. "Conflict." In *American Philosophers at Work*, edited by Sidney Hook. New York: Criterion Books, 1956.

Donagan, Alan. *The Theory of Morality*. Chicago: University of Chicago Press, 1977.

Dubs, H. H. Translator. *The Works of Hsüntze*. Taipei: Cheng-wen Publishing Co., 1966.

Emmet, Dorothy. *The Moral Prism*. London: Macmillan Press, 1979.

Fang, Thomé H. "The Essence of Wang Yang-ming's Philosophy." *Philosophy East and West*, vol. 23, nos. 1–2 (1973).

Feigl, Herbert. "Validation and Vindication." In *Readings in Ethical Theory*, edited by Wilfrid Sellars and John Hospers. New York: Appleton-Century-Crofts, 1952.

Fogelin, Robert J. *Evidence and Meaning*. London: Routledge & Kegan Paul, 1967.

Frankena, W. K. *Ethics*. 2nd ed. Englewood Cliffs: Prentice-Hall, 1973.

Frankfurt, Harry. "Freedom of the Will and the Concept of a Person." *Journal of Philosophy*, vol. 68, no. 1 (1971).

French, Peter. *The Scope of Morality*. Minneapolis: University of Minnesota Press, 1979.

Fung, Yu-lan. *A History of Chinese Philosophy*. Vol. 2. Princeton: Princeton University Press, 1953.

Geach, Peter. "Good and Evil." In *Theories of Ethics*, edited by Philippa Foot. Oxford: Oxford University Press, 1967.

Gewirth, Alan. *Reason and Morality*. Chicago: University of Chicago Press, 1978.

Graham, A. C. *Two Chinese Philosophers: Ch'eng Ming-tao and Ch'eng Yi-ch'uan*. London: Lund Humphries, 1958.

Hampshire, Stuart. *Thought and Action*. London: Chatto and Windus, 1959.

Harrison, Andrew. "Creativity and Understanding." *Proceedings of the Aristotelean Society*, suppl. vol. 41 (1971).

Henke, Frederick Goodrich. Translator. *The Philosophy of Wang Yang-ming*. New York: Paragon Book Reprint Corp., 1964.

Hintikka, Jaakko. "Practical vs. Theoretical Reason: An Ambiguous Legacy." In *Practical Reason*, edited by Stephen Körner. New Haven: Yale University Press, 1974.

James, William. *Essays in Radical Empiricism and a Pluralistic Universe.* New York: E. P. Dutton, 1971.

Karlgren, Bernard. *Analytical Dictionary of Chinese and Sino-Japanese.* Taipei: Ch'eng-wen Publishing Co., 1975.

Kierkegaard, Søren. *Concluding Unscientific Postscript.* Princeton: Princeton University Press, 1941.

———. *Purity of Heart Is to Will One Thing.* New York: Harper & Row, 1965.

Kovesi, Julius. *Moral Notions.* London: Routledge & Kegan Paul, 1967.

———. "Against the Ritual of 'Is' and 'Ought.' " In *Midwest Studies in Philosophy* (Studies in Ethical Theory), vol. 3. Morris: University of Minnesota Press, 1978.

Lau, D. C. Translator. *Mencius.* Baltimore: Penguin Books, 1970.

Legge, James. *The Chinese Classics.* Vols. 1–4. Oxford: Clarendon Press, 1939.

———. *The Li Chi or Collection of Treatises on the Rules of Propriety and Ceremonial Usages.* Delhi: Motilal Barnarsidaas, 1966.

Lewis, C. I. *An Analysis of Knowledge and Valuation.* La Salle: Open Court, 1946.

Liang, Chi-chao. *A History of Chinese Political Thought.* Taipei: Cheng-wen Publishing Co., 1968.

———. *Wang Yang-ming chih-hsing ho-i chi chao.* Taipei: Chung-hua shu-chü, 1968.

Liu, Chen-hsiu. "Yang-ming hsin-hsüeh shu-p'ing." *Annals of Philosophy,* no. 2 (1962).

Lo, Kuang. "Wang Yang-ming lun-hsin." *Yang-ming hsüeh lun-wen chih.* Taipei: Huakang, 1976.

Lucas, J. R. "The Philosophy of the Reasonable Man." *Philosophical Quarterly,* vol. 13, no. 51 (1963).

Matson, Wallace. *Sentience.* Berkeley and Los Angeles: University of California Press, 1976.

McMorran, Ian. "Late Ming Criticism of Wang Yang-ming: The Case of Wang Fu-chih." *Philosophy East and West,* vol. 23, nos. 1–2 (1973).

Melden, A. I. *Rights and Persons.* Berkeley and Los Angeles: University of California Press, 1978.

Moore, G. E. *Principia Ethica.* Cambridge: Cambridge University Press, 1969.

Mou, Tsung-san. *Hsin-ti yü hsing-ti.* Vol. 1. Taipei: Cheng-chung shu-chü, 1973.

Murdoch, Iris. *The Sovereignty of Good.* London: Routledge & Kegan Paul, 1970.

Murphy, A. E. *The Theory of Practical Reason*. La Salle: Open Court, 1965.

Needham, Joseph. *Science and Civilization in China*. Vol. 2: *History of Scientific Thought*. Cambridge: Cambridge University Press, 1962.

Nielsen, Kai. "Appealing to Reason." *Inquiry*, vol. 1 (1962).

Nivison, David. "The Problem of 'Knowledge' and 'Action' in Chinese Thought Since Wang Yang-ming." In *Studies in Chinese Thought*, edited by Arthur Wright. Chicago: University of Chicago Press, 1953.

————. "Moral Decision in Wang Yang-ming: The Problem of Chinese 'Existentialism.'" *Philosophy East and West*, vol. 23, nos. 1–2 (1973).

Pepper, S. C. *World Hypotheses*. Berkeley and Los Angeles: University of California Press, 1948.

————. *Sources of Value*. Berkeley and Los Angeles: University of California Press, 1958.

Perelman, Chaim. *The New Rhetoric and the Humanities: Essays on Rhetoric and Its Applications*. Dordrecht: D. Reidel, 1979.

Phillips, D. Z. and Mounce, H. O. *Moral Practices*. London: Routledge & Kegan Paul, 1969.

Rawls, John. "Outline of a Decision Procedure for Ethics." *Philosophical Review*, vol. 60, no. 2 (1951).

Reid, Thomas. *Essays on the Active Powers of the Human Mind*. Cambridge: M.I.T. Press, 1969.

Rescher, Nicholas. "Reasoned Justification of Moral Judgments." *Journal of Philosophy*, vol. 55, no. 6 (1958).

————. "On the Characterization of Actions." In *The Nature of Human Action*, edited by Myles Brand. Glenview: Scott, Foresman & Co., 1970.

Richard, Norman. "On Seeing Things Differently." In *The Philosophy of Society*, edited by Rodger Beehler and Alan R. Drengson. London: Methuen, 1978.

Ross, W. D. *The Right and the Good*. Oxford: Clarendon Press, 1930.

Russell, Bertrand. *Problems of Philosophy*. Oxford: Oxford University Press, 1950.

Ryle, Gilbert. "Conscience and Moral Convictions." In *Collected Papers, 1929–1968*. Vol. 2. London: Hutchinson & Co., 1971.

Saw, Ruth. *Aesthetics*. New York: Anchor Books, 1971.

Sibley, W. H. "The Rational vs. the Reasonable." *Philosophical Review*, vol. 62, no. 4 (1953).

T'ang, Chün-i. *Chung-Kuo che-hsüeh yüan-lun, tao-lun p'ien*. 3rd ed. Taipei: Hsüeh-sheng shu-chü, 1978.

Taylor, Charles. "Responsibility for Self." In *The Identities of Persons*, edited by Amelie Rorty. Berkeley and Los Angeles: University of California Press, 1976.

————. "What Is Human Agency?" In *The Self: Psychological and Philosophical Issues*, edited by Theodore Mischel. Oxford: Basil Blackwell, 1977.

Tolstoy, Leo. *The Death of Ivan Ilych*. New York: New American Library, 1960.

Tu, Wei-ming. *Neo-Confucian Thought in Action: Wang Yang-ming's Youth (1472–1509)*. Berkeley and Los Angeles: University of California Press, 1976.

Wang, Hsien-ch'ien. *Hsün Tzu chih-chieh*. Taipei: Shih-chieh shu-chü, n.d.

Wang, Yang-ming. *Wang Yang-ming ch'uan-shu*. 4 vols. Taipei: Cheng Chung Book Co., 1955.

Watson, Burton. Translator. *Hsün Tzu: Basic Writings*. New York: Columbia University Press, 1963.

Weiss, Paul. *You, I, and the Others*. Carbondale: Southern Illinois University Press, 1980.

Wheelwright, Philip. *The Burning Fountain: A Study in the Language of Symbolism*. Bloomington: Indiana University Press, 1968.

Wiggens, David. "Deliberation and Practical Reason." *Proceedings of the Aristotelean Society*, NS 76 (1975–1976).

Williams, Bernard. *Problems of the Self*. Cambridge: Cambridge University Press, 1973.

Winch, Peter. *Ethics and Action*. London: Routledge & Kegan Paul, 1972.

Wittgenstein, Ludwig. *Philosophical Investigations*. 3rd ed. New York: Macmillan, 1969.

Zweig, Stefan. "Transfiguration." In *The World of Psychoanalysis*, edited by G. B. Levitas. Vol. 2. New York: George Braziller, 1965.

Glossary

Chan Wing-tsit　陳榮捷
Chang Tsai　張載
chen-chih　眞知
Cheng Chung-ying　成中英
ch'eng　誠
Ch'eng Hao　程顥
Ch'eng I　程頤
ch'eng-yi　誠意
chi　卽
chiang-chiu　講求
chih　知
chih-hsing ho-i　知行合一
chih-shan　至善
chih*　志
chin-ssu　近思
ching　敬
Chu Tzu　朱子
Ch'uan hsi-lu　傳習錄
chung　中
chung*　忠
Chung Yung　中庸
chu-yi　主意
Confucius　孔夫子
fa　發
Fei-hsiang p'ien　非相篇

ho　和
ho-i　合一
hsiao　孝
hsien　顯
hsin　心
hsin-chi-li*　心卽理
hsing　行
Hsü Ai　徐愛
hsüeh-hsing ho-i　學行合一
Hsün Tzu　荀子
i　義
i-chih*　意志
i-li*　義理
jen　仁
ko-wu　格物
kung ming　共名
kung-fu　工夫
Kuo Hsiang　郭象
li　禮
li*　理
li-chih*　立志
li*-yu　理由
Liang Chi-chao　梁啓超
liang-chih　良知
ling-ch'u　靈處

ling-ming　靈明
ling-neng　靈能
Liu Chen-hsiu　劉珍修
Lo Kuang　羅光
lun　倫
Mencius　孟子
Mou Tsung-san　牟宗三
nien　念
pen-ti　本體
pi　蔽
pieh ming　別名
sheng　聖
shih　事
shih*　視
shu　恕
Shun　舜
szu-yü　私欲
Ta Hsüeh　大學
T'ang Chün-i　唐君毅
tao　道

tao-li*　道理
tao wu chung-ch'ung　道無終窮
ti　體
t'iao-li*　條理
t'ien　天
t'ien-li*　天理
t'ou-nao　頭腦
Tu Wei-ming　杜維明
tung　動
Tzu-hsia　子夏
Wang Hsien-ch'ien　王先謙
Wang Yang-ming　王陽明
wen　文
wu　物
yi　意
yi-chih*　意志
yi-i pien-ying　以義變應
yin　隱
yin-shih chi-i　因時制宜
yü　欲

Index

⊞ Production Notes

This book was designed by Roger Eggers.

Composition and paging were done on the
Quadex Composing System and typesetting on
the Compugraphic Unisetter. The text typeface
is Compugraphic Caledonia and the display
typeface is Paladium.

Offset presswork and binding were done by
Halliday Lithograph. Text paper is Glatfelter
Offset, basis 55.